Santa's Great Book

LEISURE ARTS, INC.
and
OXMOOR HOUSE, INC.

Santa's Great Book

EDITORIAL STAFF

Vice President and Editor-in-Chief:
Anne Van Wagner Childs
Executive Director: Sandra Graham Case
Executive Editor: Susan Frantz Wiles
Publications Director: Carla Bentley
Creative Art Director: Gloria Bearden
Production Art Director: Melinda Stout

EDITORIAL
Associate Editor: Linda L. Trimble
Senior Editorial Writer: Darla Burdette Kelsay
Editorial Writer: Robyn Sheffield-Edwards
Editorial Associates: Tammi Williamson Bradley
and Terri Leming Davidson
Copy Editor: Laura Lee Weland

TECHNICAL
Managing Editor: Lisa Truxton Curton
Senior Editor: Laura Siar Holyfield
Senior Production Coordinator:
Connie White Irby

ART
Book/Magazine Art Director: Diane M. Hugo
Senior Production Artist: Brent Jones
Photography Stylists: Laura Bushmiaer,
Sondra Daniel, Karen Hall, Aurora Huston,
Emily Minnick, Christina Tiano Myers,
and Zaneta Senger

BUSINESS STAFF

Publisher: Bruce Akin
Vice President, Finance: Tom Siebenmorgen
Vice President, Retail Sales: Thomas L. Carlisle
Retail Sales Director: Richard Tignor
Vice President, Retail Marketing: Pam Stebbins
Retail Customer Services Director: Margaret Sweetin
General Merchandise Manager: Russ Barnett

Distribution Director: Ed M. Strackbein
Executive Director of Marketing and Circulation:
Guy A. Crossley
Circulation Manager: Byron L. Taylor
Print Production Manager: Laura Lockhart
Print Production Coordinator: Nancy Reddick Baker

Library of Congress Catalog Number 96-75335
Hardcover ISBN 1-57486-040-2
Softcover ISBN 1-57486-039-9

Introduction

At last — all together in one irresistible book — here are your favorite Santa designs from Leisure Arts leaflets and magazines! As you browse through the pages of Santa's Great Book, *you'll be whisked away to the wonderful world of Santa Claus as seen through the eyes of both modern and turn-of-the-century artists. Recognized around the world by many names, the legendary gift-giver is portrayed as Kris Kringle, St. Nicholas, Father Christmas, and more. There are also enchanting scenes that depict the rosy-cheeked fellow in his toy shop, spreading holiday cheer, and making his Christmas Eve journey. And you'll be delighted by his ever-changing mythical travel companions! Many of the heirloom images are shown custom framed, but we've also given lots of exciting ideas for displaying them on afghans, pillows, stockings, and more. May* Santa's Great Book *inspire you to keep on believing!*

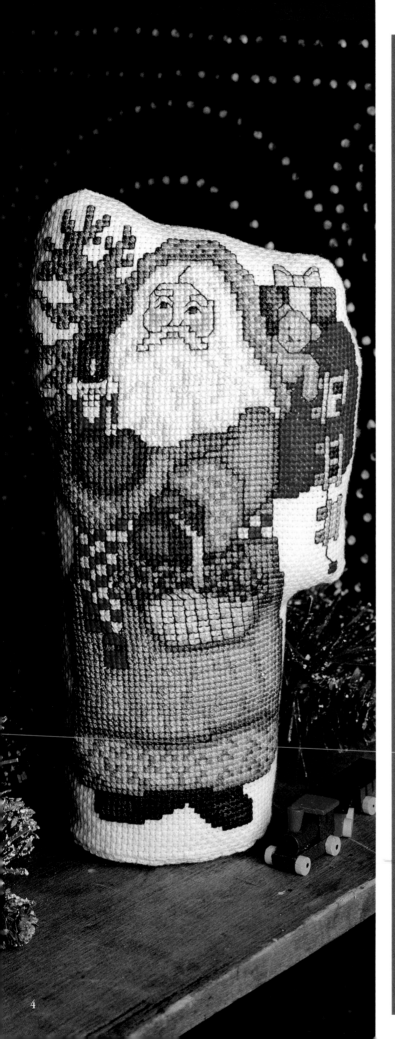

Table

of Contents

Chart on pages 70-71

Traveling Companions

Santa Claus is traditionally depicted making his Christmas Eve journey in a beautiful sleigh drawn by eight prancing reindeer. But through the years, artists have paired the legendary gift-giver with a variety of mythical traveling companions — from majestic horses to ponderous polar bears. He's even captured riding on the back of a stately snow owl in this enchanting collection.

Chart on pages 74-75

Chart on pages 72-73

Chart on pages 76-77

We ride to you on steeds so fleeting,
To bring a cordial Christmas greeting.

— FROM AN ANTIQUE POSTCARD

Chart on pages 76-77

The Enchanted Sleigh

With a majestic angel at the helm to guide the way and a heavenly cherub to bless the journey, St. Nicholas makes his Christmas Eve deliveries from his enchanted sleigh.

Chart on pages 78-79

Christmas Journey

In this woodland scene, Santa makes his Christmas journey the old-fashioned way — on foot! With the aid of his trusty staff, he treks through the wintry landscape with only a lantern to light his way.

Chart on pages 80-81

CLASSIC OLDE SANTAS

Each of the Olde Santas in this classic collection first appeared on the covers of Leisure Arts The Magazine. *The beloved series began in the December 1986 issue and continues today to capture the many faces of Santa Claus. Sized especially for framing, the portraits can also be used to create a variety of projects, from stockings and tree skirts to afghans and mantel cloths.*

Chart on page 87

Chart on page 83

Christmas is here, Merry old Christmas,
Gift-bearing, heart-touching, Joy-bringing Christmas,
Day of grand memories, King of the year!

— WASHINGTON IRVING

Chart on page 86

Chart on page 86

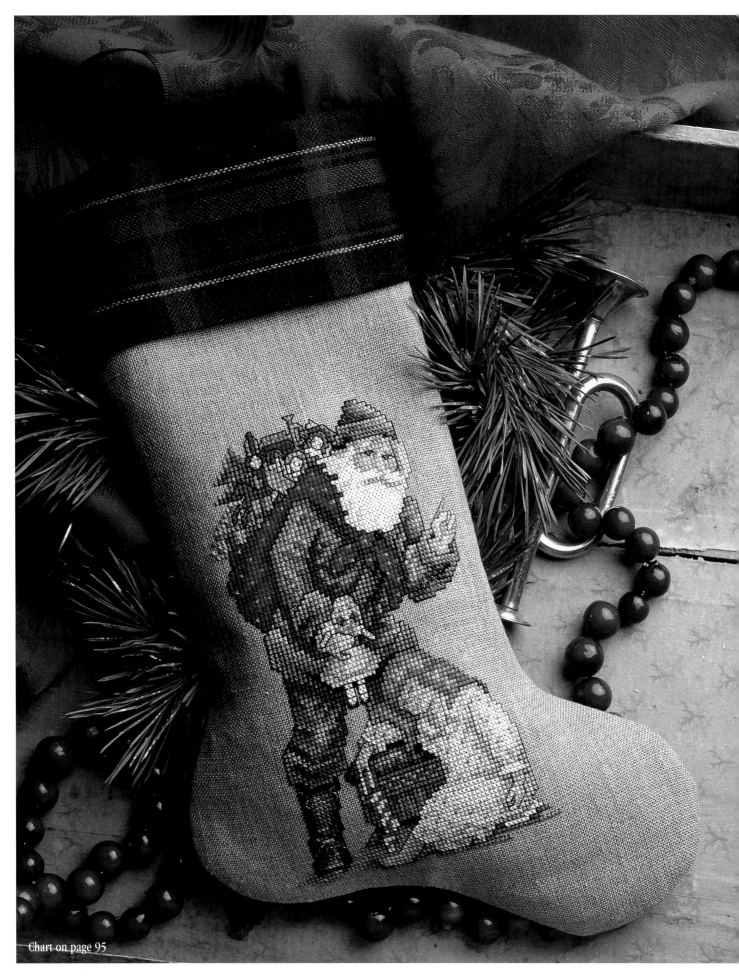

Chart on page 95

If Santa dropped his choicest gifts
On Christmas morning down your flue
I still should think he had not brought
Quite all the joys deserved by you!

— FROM AN ANTIQUE POSTCARD

Chart on page 95

Never deny the babies their Christmas! It is the shining seal set upon a year
of happiness. Let them believe in Santa Claus, or St. Nicholas, or Kriss Kringle,
or whatever name the jolly Dutch saint bears in your religion.

— MARION HARLAND

Chart on page 87

Chart on page 91

He comes — the brave old Christmas! His sturdy steps I hear;
We will give him a hearty welcome, For he comes but once a year!

— MARY HOWITT

Chart on page 97

Chart on page 89

Chart on page 85

Chart on page 93

St. Nick's prowling around in the snow,
While you're snuggling comfy and all aglow,
He's headed straight for your own house,
And in he'll steal as quiet as a mouse.

— FROM AN ANTIQUE POSTCARD

Chart on page 94

Chart on page 94

WHITE CHRISTMAS

*As Santa travels quietly through a snowy forest, he shares his
holiday wish of peace and good will with a gentle bird and rabbit.
Whether framed or finished as a pillow, this design will give
any room a wonderful Olde World feeling.*

Chart on pages 98-99

Chart on pages 98-99

Straight to His Work

Months of preparation and planning take place before Santa can go to work filling stockings and making his Christmas Eve deliveries. First he diligently records the names of all the good little girls and boys in his great book, then he undertakes the task of constructing their toys in his workshop! Our trio of portraits shows his devotion to all three phases of his work.

Chart on pages 100-101

Chart on pages 102-105

There's nothing Santa more enjoys
Than making toys for girls and boys.
And in his way, he's wondrous wise,
For he knows just what'll please your eyes.

— FROM AN ANTIQUE POSTCARD

Chart on pages 106-107

HO-HO PILLOWS

These festive throw pillows feature two portraits of Santa. One was inspired by the closing line of Clement Clarke Moore's "The Night Before Christmas," and the other shows St. Nick welcoming the holidays with a sporting theme.

Chart on page 109

Chart on page 108

Chart on pages 110-111

MILES TO GO

Knowing of the untraveled miles that lie ahead, Santa takes a short rest on his long journey to enjoy a wintry repast.

And Then, in a Twinkling

This enchanting Yuletide portrait was inspired by a familiar verse from "The Night Before Christmas." Loaded down with a sack full of toys, the jolly old chap congratulates Dasher, the leader of the reindeer team, on another perfect housetop landing.

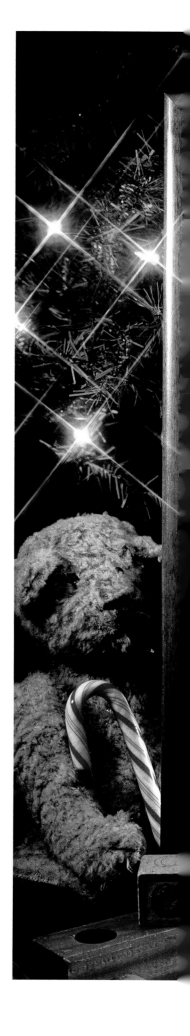

Chart on pages 112-113

Santa Reunion

Over the centuries, Santa has been depicted in many shapes, sizes, and forms, but he has remained steadfast as a deliverer of happiness and joy. We've gathered some of our all-time favorite fellows — from Father Christmas to an Uncle Sam St. Nick — for the jolliest Yuletide reunion ever!

Chart on pages 114-115

GOOD CHEER

Unloading his bag full of Yuletide joys, our Olde World Santa brings good cheer to all girls and boys. This beautiful design captures the true giving spirit of the holiday season.

Chart on pages 116-117

PRAIRIE SANTA

Riding high atop a holiday holstein, our Prairie Santa pays tribute to the American farmer. The whimsical gent is appropriately dressed in overalls and work boots, and he carries a pitchfork and a sack of down-home gifts.

Chart on pages 118-121

BE JOLLY

Charts on pages 122-123

BE JOLLY

Inspired by a holiday character from the Netherlands, our Sinterklaas expresses a simple holiday sentiment that's worth sharing — Be Jolly! It's only fitting that the merry elf is dressed in a suit embellished with hearts and flowers and that his bag of toys includes a miniature windmill and a provincial doll.

BY THE LIGHT OF THE MOON

*Inspired by the moon that lights his way, this crescent-shaped
Santa looks radiant fashioned as an accent pillow. A rich blue afghan,
reminiscent of the midnight sky, makes a striking backdrop
for Santa and his team of reindeer.*

Chart on page 124

Chart on pages 126-127

A Visit
from Santa

Christmas Eve is a time of joyful expectation, when every little sound seems to signal Santa's arrival. With hearts aflutter, eager youngsters rush to the window again and again, hoping to get a glimpse of that dear old man and all the gifts he has in store for them.

Chart on pages 128-129

JOYFUL SANTA

*With a message of joy to lead him and a candle to light his
way, this American Santa travels toward his next destination.
A fur-lined coat protects him from the snowy night as he
delivers toys and other gifts to eager boys and girls.*

Chart on pages 130-131

Chart on pages 130-131

FOR YOU

A gentle St. Nicholas offers a kindly smile and a beribboned teddy just for you. This beautifully detailed design will add old-fashioned charm to your holiday decor, whether framed or finished as a tree skirt.

Chart on page 132

Chart on page 132

Santa's Toyshop Bears

A hole in Santa's knapsack provides an escape route for a band of wayfaring windup bears in this whimsical design. Stitched on an afghan, the playful scene will wrap you in the magic of Christmas.

Chart on page 133

YOU BETTER NOT POUT

Santa seems to be reminding us that he knows who's been naughty or nice in this nostalgic design, yet his gentle expression reflects the kindness and generosity that has inspired generations of children to "be good for goodness' sake." Stitched on an afghan or framed, this delightful image of Santa is sure to become a family heirloom.

Chart on page 125

Chart on page 125

MERRY GENTLEMEN

Three gift-bringers from around the world come together in this design to offer a universal "Merry Christmas." Each Santa also makes an enchanting doll.

Chart on pages 134-135

Turn-of-the-Century Santa

Dressed in a rich blue coat, this Santa Claus was inspired by a turn-of-the-century image. Certain to become an heirloom, he overflows with vintage Christmas charm. And because his rosy-cheeked face is so irresistible, we captured his features on an ornament and stocking, too!

Chart on page 136

Chart on page 136

Old St. Nick

Laden with presents to delight children of all ages, St. Nicholas embodies the generosity of the Yuletide season. The Christmas gentleman adds Olde World charm to a keepsake gift bag, or he can be fashioned as a decorative doll for an endearing accent.

Chart on page 137

Chart on page 137

DEAR SANTA

This poignant letter to Santa captures the special relationship between a child and the jolly Christmas visitor. The design was stitched on blue fabric to enhance the moonlit scene.

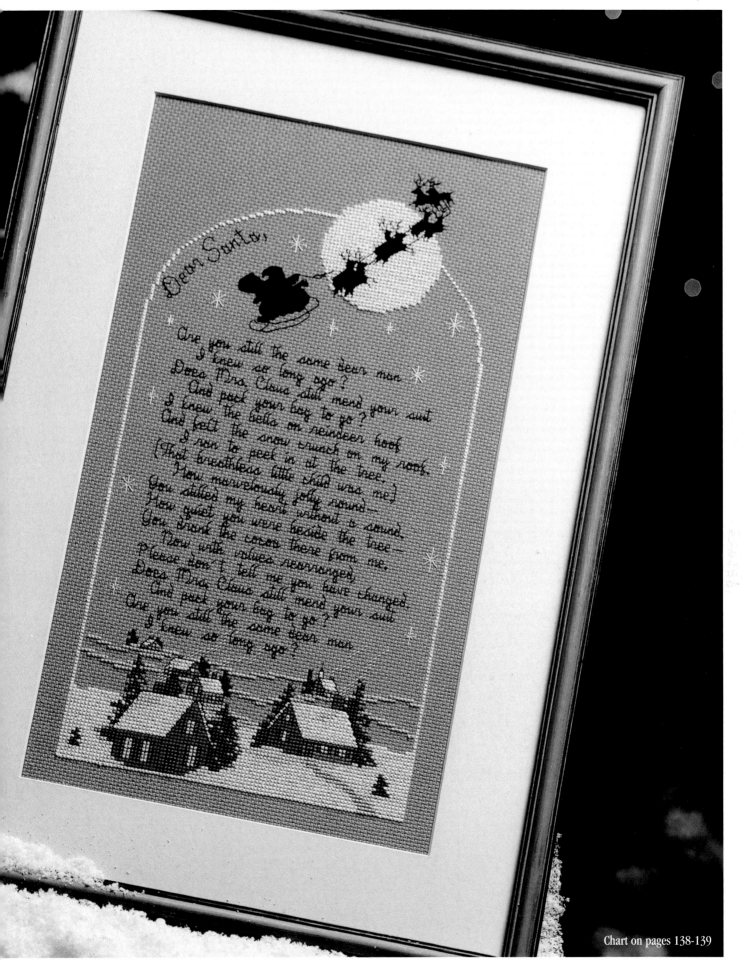

Chart on pages 138-139

SANTA AND HORSE (120w x 144h)

Aida 11	11"	x	13 1/8"
Aida 14	8 5/8"	x	10 3/8"
Aida 18	6 3/4"	x	8"
Hardanger 22	5 1/2"	x	6 5/8"

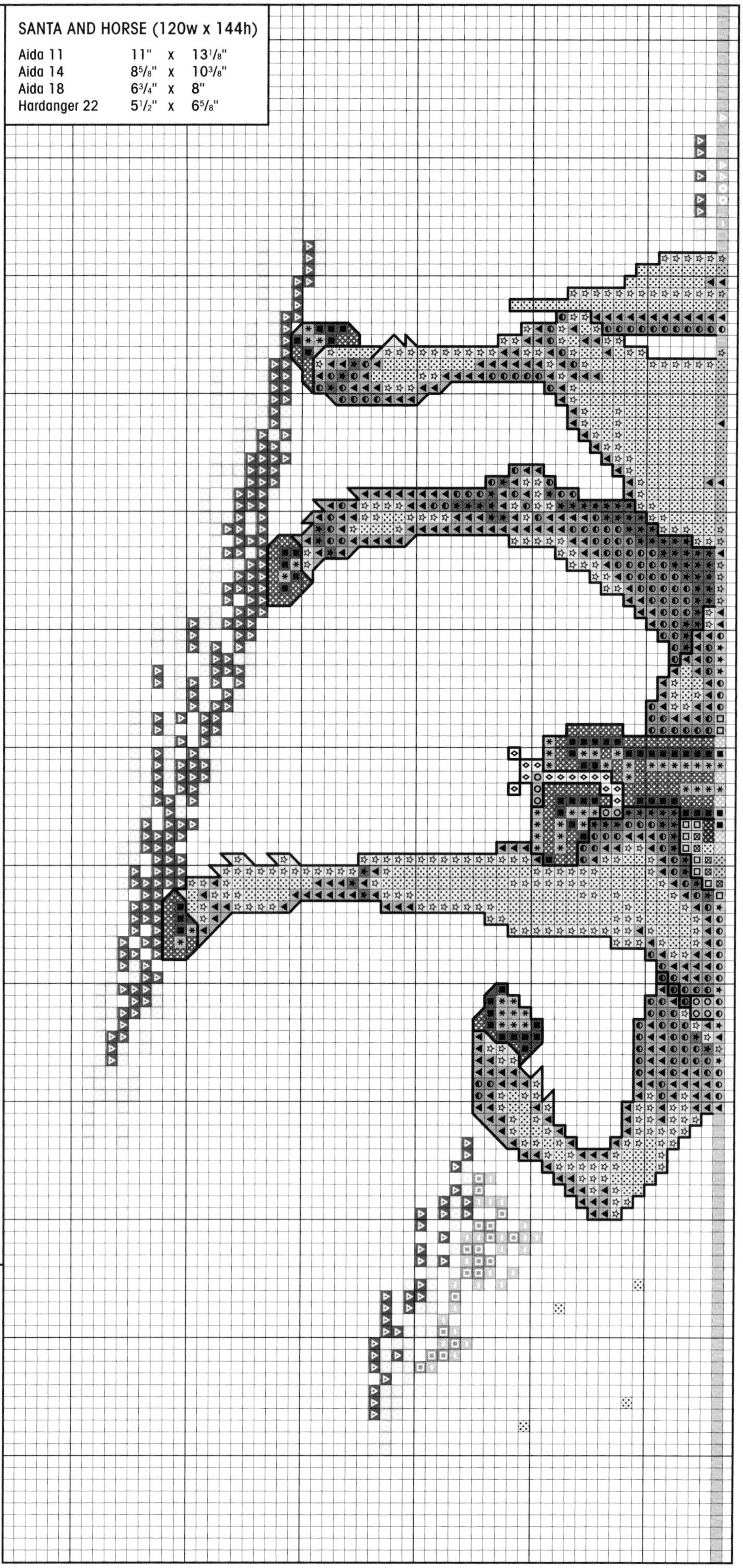

SANTA AND HORSE (120w x 144h)

DMC	1/4X	1/2X	B'ST	ANC	COLOR
blanc	■	■		2	white
300				352	dk rust
301				1049	lt rust
310	■		■	403	black
315				1019	vy dk mauve
316				1017	mauve
400				351	rust
413	■			401	grey
543				933	beige
640			■	903	vy dk beige brown
642	■			392	dk beige brown
644	■			830	beige brown
648			■	900	lt grey
725	■			305	yellow
754	■			1012	peach

DMC	1/4X	B'ST	ANC.	COLOR
758	■		882	flesh
760			1022	lt salmon
778			968	vy lt mauve
782			308	gold
783			307	lt gold
822	■		390	lt beige brown
838			380	vy dk brown
839			360	dk brown
840	■		379	brown
841	■	■	378	lt brown
842			388	vy lt brown
895			1044	dk green
926			850	grey blue
927			848	lt grey blue
928			274	vy lt grey blue

DMC	1/4X	1/2X	B'ST	ANC.	COLOR
962				75	pink
3064	■			883	dk flesh
3328				1024	dk salmon
3345		■		268	green
3346		■	■	267	lt green
3712				1023	salmon
3721	■			896	dk rose
3722				1027	rose
3726				1018	dk mauve
3727				1016	lt mauve
3768		■		779	dk grey blue
3779	■			868	lt flesh
3799	■			236	dk grey

Pink area indicates last row of top section of design.

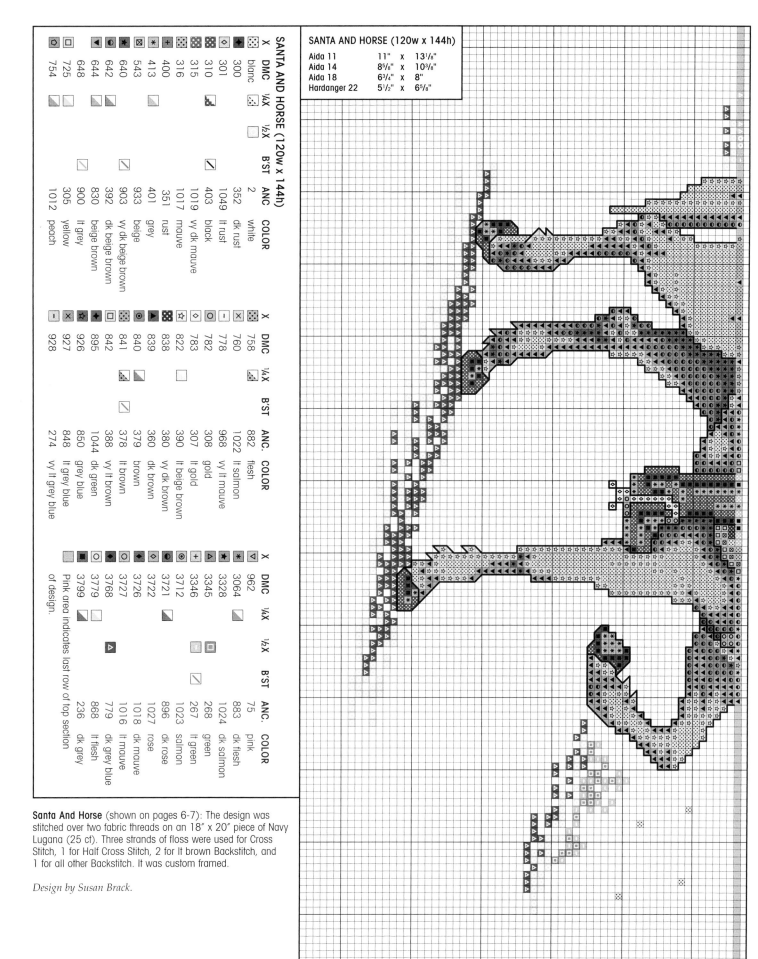

Santa And Horse (shown on pages 6-7): The design was stitched over two fabric threads on an 18" x 20" piece of Navy Lugana (25 ct). Three strands of floss were used for Cross Stitch, 1 for Half Cross Stitch, 2 for lt brown Backstitch, and 1 for all other Backstitch. It was custom framed.

Design by Susan Brack.

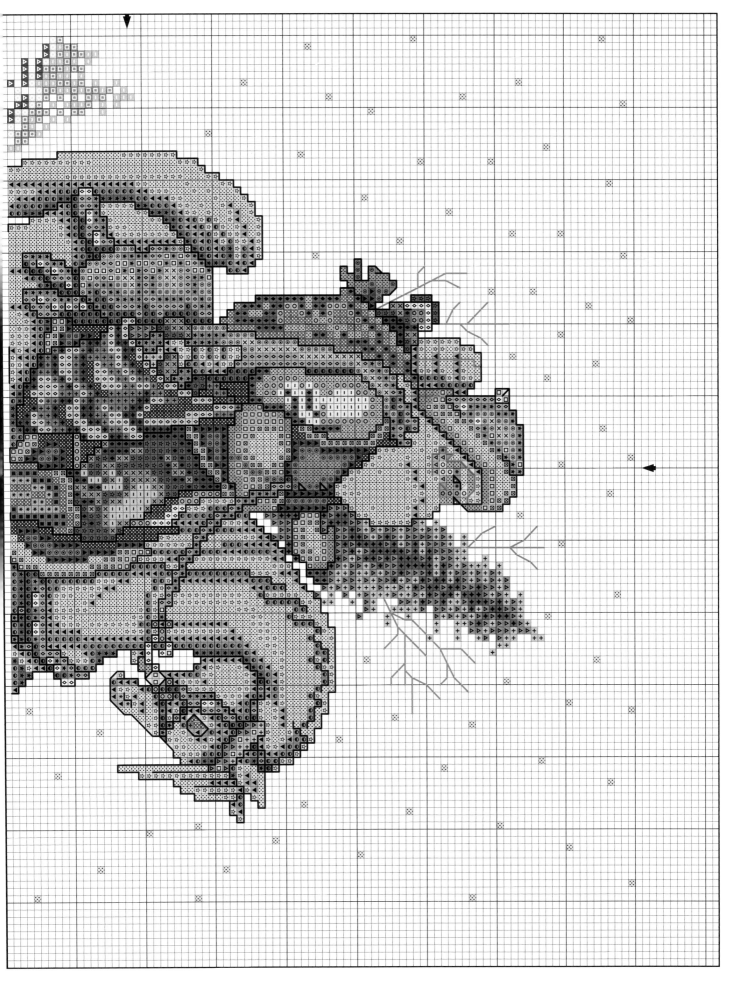

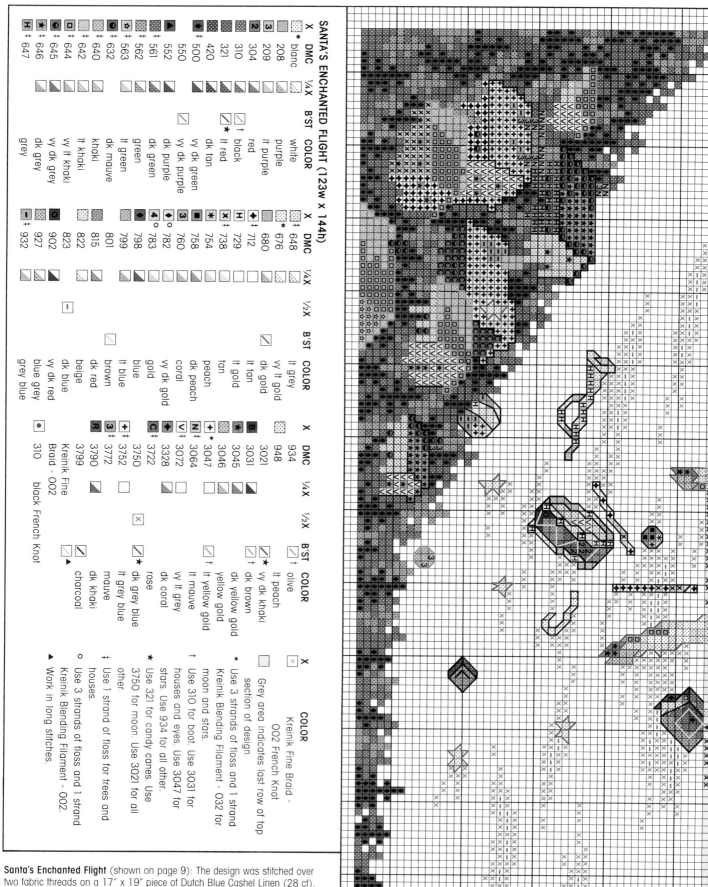

SANTA'S ENCHANTED FLIGHT (123w x 144h)

X	¼X	B'ST	DMC	COLOR
			blanc	white
			208	purple
			209	lt purple
			304	red
			310	black
			321	lt red
			420	dk tan
			500	vy dk green
			550	vy dk purple
			552	dk purple
			561	dk green
			562	green
			563	lt green
			632	dk mauve
			640	khaki
			642	lt khaki
			644	vy lt khaki
			645	vy dk grey
			646	dk grey
			647	grey

X	¼X	½X	B'ST	DMC	COLOR
				648	lt grey
				676	vy lt gold
				680	dk gold
				712	lt tan
				729	tan
				738	lt gold
				754	peach
				758	dk peach
				760	coral
				782	vy dk gold
				783	gold
				798	blue
				799	lt blue
				801	brown
				815	dk red
				822	beige
				823	dk blue
				902	vy dk red
				927	blue grey
				932	grey blue

X	¼X	½X	B'ST	DMC	COLOR
				934	olive
				948	vy dk khaki
				3021	dk brown
				3031	vy dk khaki
				3045	dk yellow gold
				3046	yellow gold
				3047	lt yellow gold
				3064	lt mauve
				3072	vy lt grey
				3328	dk coral
				3722	rose
				3750	dk grey blue
				3752	lt grey blue
				3772	mauve
				3790	dk khaki
				3799	charcoal
				Kreinik Fine Braid - 002	
				310	black French Knot

X   COLOR
Kreinik Fine Braid - 002 French Knot

□   Grey area indicates last row of top section of design.

*   Use 3 strands of floss and 1 strand Kreinik Blending Filament - 032 for moon and stars.

†   Use 310 for boot. Use 3031 for houses and eyes. Use 3047 for stars. Use 934 for all other.

★   Use 321 for candy canes. Use 3750 for moon. Use 3021 for all other.

‡   Use 1 strand of floss for houses.

○   Use 3 strands of floss and 1 strand Kreinik Blending Filament - 002.

▶   Work in long stitches.

Santa's Enchanted Flight (shown on page 9): The design was stitched over two fabric threads on a 17" x 19" piece of Dutch Blue Cashel Linen (28 ct). Three strands of floss were used for Cross Stitch, and 1 for Half Cross Stitch, Backstitch (unless otherwise indicated in color key), and French Knots. It was custom framed.

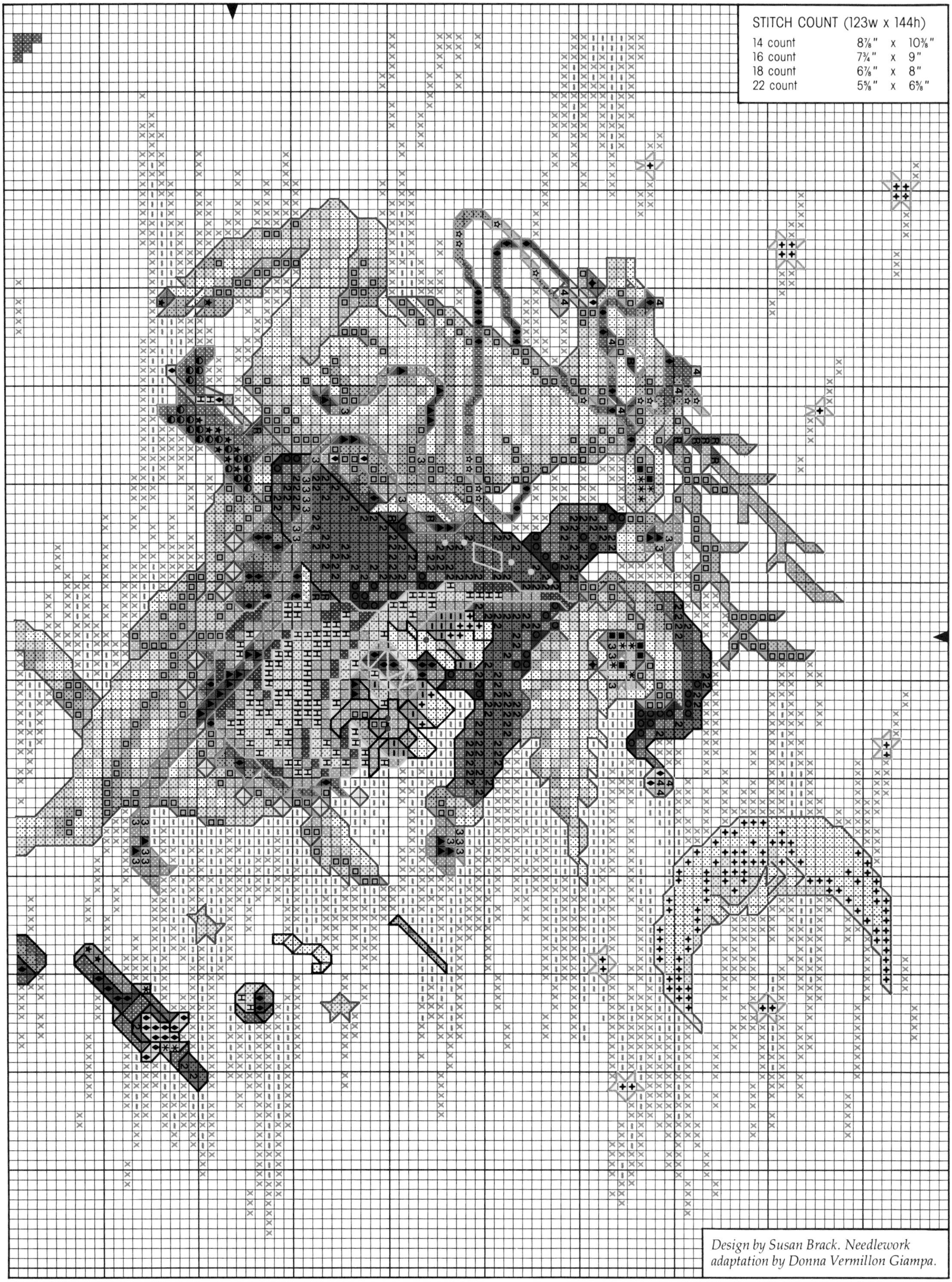

STITCH COUNT (123w x 144h)

14 count	8⅞"	x	10⅜"
16 count	7¾"	x	9"
18 count	6⅞"	x	8"
22 count	5⅝"	x	6⅝"

Design by Susan Brack. Needlework adaptation by Donna Vermillon Giampa.

Santa And Bear (shown on page 8): The design was stitched over two fabric threads on an 18″ x 20″ piece of Navy Lugana (25 ct). Three strands of floss were used for Cross Stitch, 1 for Half Cross Stitch, 2 for lt brown Backstitch, and 1 for all other Backstitch. It was custom framed.

Design by Susan Brack.

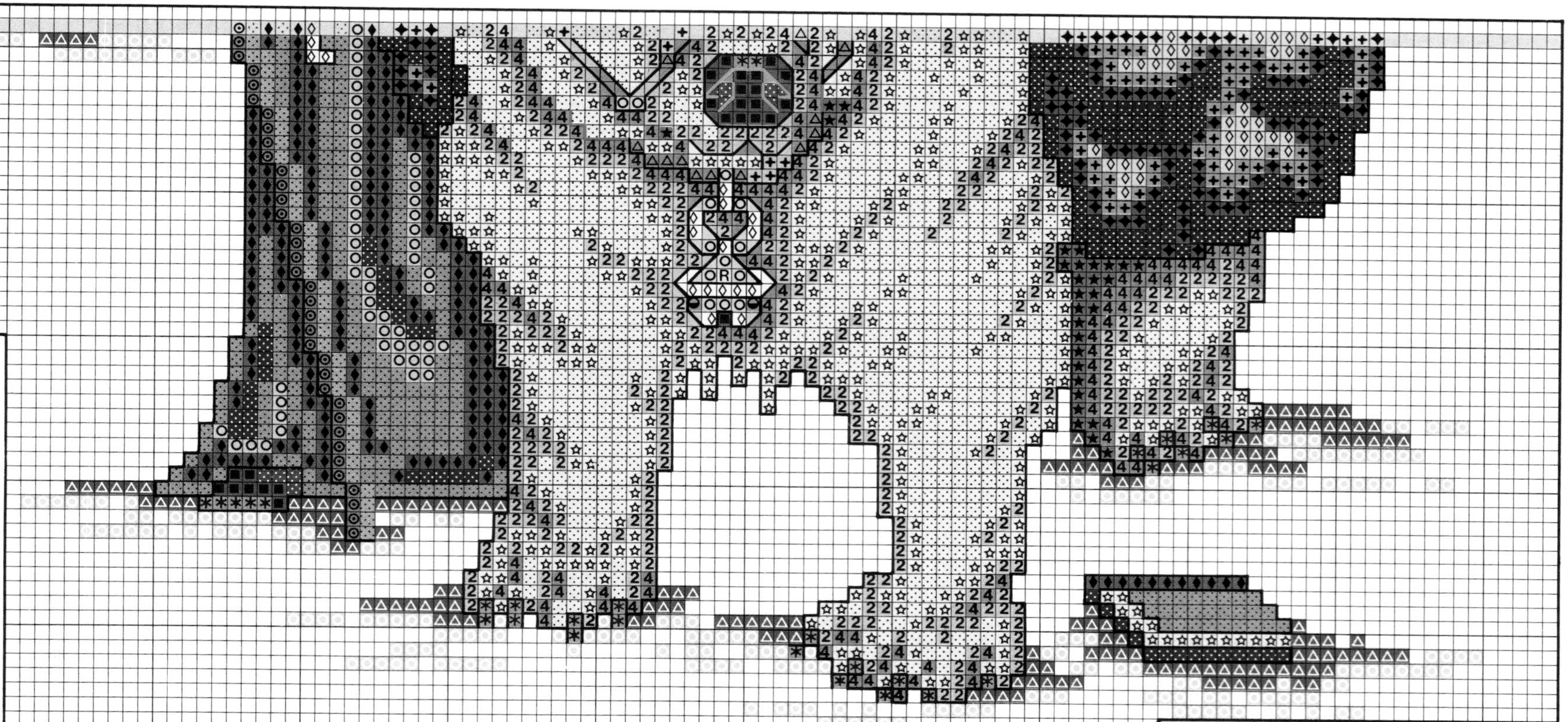

SANTA AND BEAR (115w x 138h)			
Aida 11	$10\frac{1}{2}''$	x	$12\frac{5}{8}''$
Aida 14	$8\frac{1}{4}''$	x	$9\frac{7}{8}''$
Aida 18	$6\frac{1}{2}''$	x	$7\frac{3}{4}''$
Hardanger 22	$5\frac{1}{4}''$	x	$6\frac{3}{8}''$

SANTA AND BEAR (115w x 138h)

X	DMC	¼X	½X	B'ST	JPC	COLOR
	blanc				1001	white
	300					dk rust
	301					lt rust
	310				8403	black
	315				3082	vy dk mauve
	316				3081	mauve
	400					rust
	413				8514	grey
C	543				5533	beige
	610				5889	taupe
	640				5393	vy dk beige brown
4	642				5832	dk beige brown
2	644				5831	beige brown
	648				8390	lt grey

X	DMC	¼X	B'ST	JPC	COLOR
R	725			2298	yellow
H	754			3146	peach
	758			3868	flesh
	780				dk gold
	782			5308	gold
	783			5307	lt gold
	822			5830	lt beige brown
	838			5381	vy dk brown
	839			5360	dk brown
	840			5379	brown
	841			5578	lt brown
	842			5933	vy lt brown
	895			6021	dk green
	926			6007	grey blue

X	DMC	¼X	½X	JPC	COLOR
	927			6006	lt grey blue
	928			7225	vy lt grey blue
A	962			3151	pink
	3064			3883	dk flesh
	3345			6258	green
	3346			6258	lt green
	3347			6266	vy lt green
	3726			3084	dk mauve
	3727				lt mauve
	3768				dk grey blue
V	3779				lt flesh
	3799			8999	dk grey

Purple area indicates last row of top section of design.

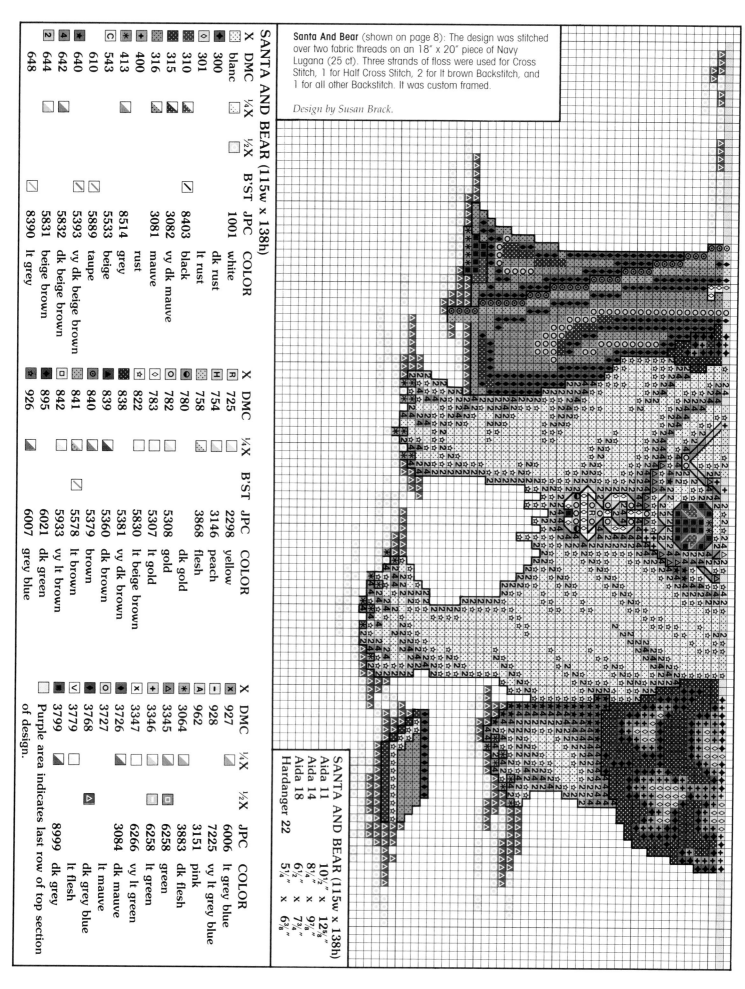

ST. NICHOLAS AND SNOW OWL (91w x 126h)

X	1/4X	B'ST	DMC	JPC	COLOR
			blanc	1001	white
			311	7980	vy dk blue
			312	7979	dk blue
			317	8512	dk grey
			318	8511	grey
			319	6246	dk green
			320	6017	lt green
			322	7978	blue
			347	3013	lt red
			367	6018	green
			368	6016	vy lt green
			413	8514	vy dk grey
			415	8398	lt grey

X	1/4X	B'ST	DMC	JPC	COLOR
			498	3410	red
			610	5889	dk brown
			611	5898	brown
			612		lt brown
			613		vy lt brown
			725	2298	lt gold
			754	2331	lt flesh
			758	3868	flesh
			762	8510	vy lt grey
			782	5308	dk gold
			783	5307	gold
			813	7161	lt blue
			814	3044	dk red

X	1/4X	B'ST	DMC	JPC	COLOR
			890	6021	vy dk green
			902	3083	dk mauve
			3031	5472	vy dk brown
			3064	3883	dk flesh
			3328	3071	vy lt red
			3371	5478	brown black
			3685	3089	mauve
			3687	3089	lt mauve
			3712	3088	pink

Grey area indicates last row of top section of design.

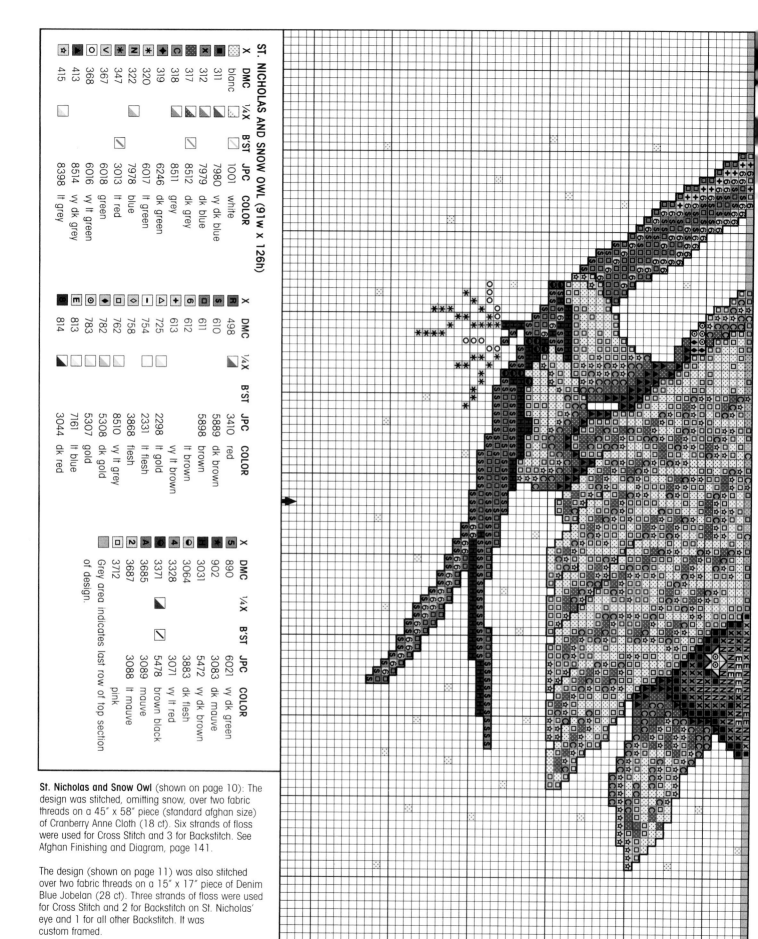

St. Nicholas and Snow Owl (shown on page 10): The design was stitched, omitting snow, over two fabric threads on a 45" x 58" piece (standard afghan size) of Cranberry Anne Cloth (18 ct). Six strands of floss were used for Cross Stitch and 3 for Backstitch. See Afghan Finishing and Diagram, page 141.

The design (shown on page 11) was also stitched over two fabric threads on a 15" x 17" piece of Denim Blue Jobelan (28 ct). Three strands of floss were used for Cross Stitch and 2 for Backstitch on St. Nicholas' eye and 1 for all other Backstitch. It was custom framed.

Design by Susan Brack.

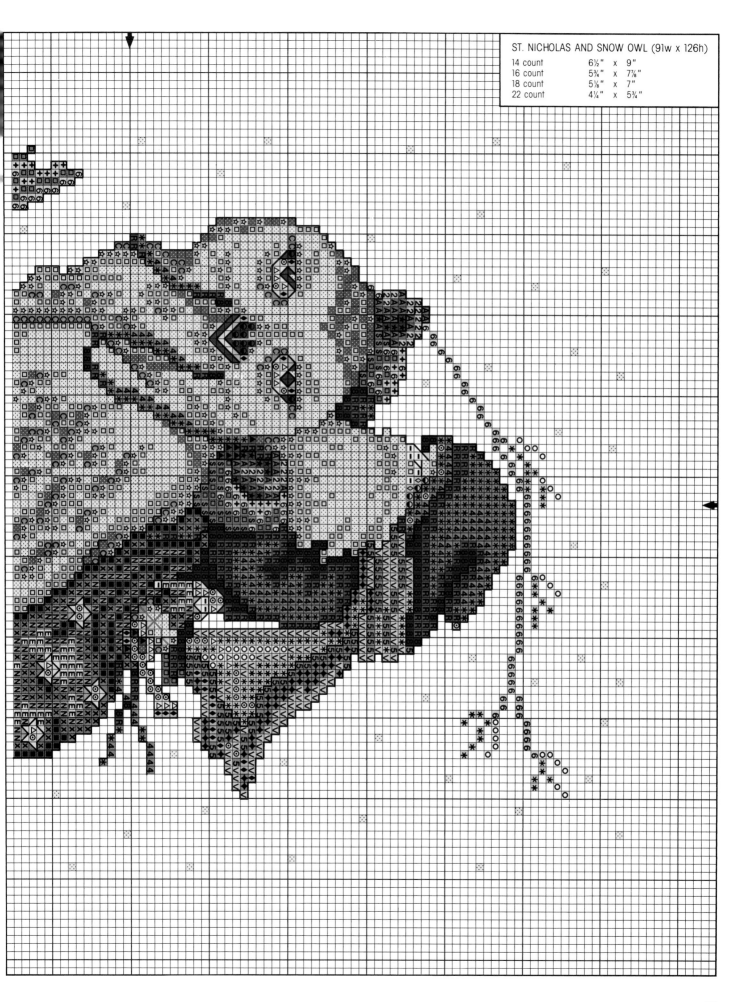

ST. NICHOLAS AND SNOW OWL (91w x 126h)

14 count	6½"	x 9"
16 count	5¾"	x 7⅞"
18 count	5⅛"	x 7"
22 count	4¼"	x 5¾"

ENCHANTED SLEIGH (136w x 96h)

X	DMC	¼X	½X	B'ST	JPC	COLOR
▨	blanc	▨	▨		1001	white
V	347				3013	red
★	498	◩			3410	dk red
▲	501	◩			6878	dk blue green
◉	502	◩			6876	blue green
△	503	☐			6879	lt blue green
◆	640			◩	5393	dk beige grey
▨	642				5832	beige grey
✚	644	◩			5831	lt beige grey
▨	725	▨			2298	yellow
○	727				2289	lt yellow
☐	754	☐			3146	lt flesh
✳	758	◩			3868	dk flesh
▨	780	◪				dk gold
◉	781	◩			5309	gold
✕	783	☐			5307	lt gold
▨	814	◪			3044	maroon
−	822	☐			5830	vy lt beige grey
◆	839	◩			5360	brown
▲	902				3083	dk maroon
★	935	◩			6270	dk green
▨	962	▨			3151	pink
▨	3064	◪			3883	vy dk flesh
◇	3328				3071	lt red
4	3362	◪			6318	green
2	3363				6317	lt green
☆	3364				6010	vy lt green
	3371			◩	5478	brown black
■	3685	◪			3089	dk mauve
☆	3687				3088	mauve
△	3779	☐				flesh
▨	Blue area indicates last row of right side of design.					

ENCHANTED SLEIGH (136w x 96h)

Aida 11	12³/₈"	x	8³/₄"	
Aida 14	9³/₄"	x	6⁷/₈"	
Aida 18	7⁵/₈"	x	5³/₈"	
Hardanger 22	6¹/₄"	x	4³/₈"	

The Enchanted Sleigh (shown on pages 12-13): The design was stitched over two fabric threads on an 18" x 15" piece of Denim Blue Jobelan (28 ct). Three strands of floss were used for Cross Stitch and 1 for Half Cross Stitch and Backstitch. It was custom framed.

Design by Susan Brack.

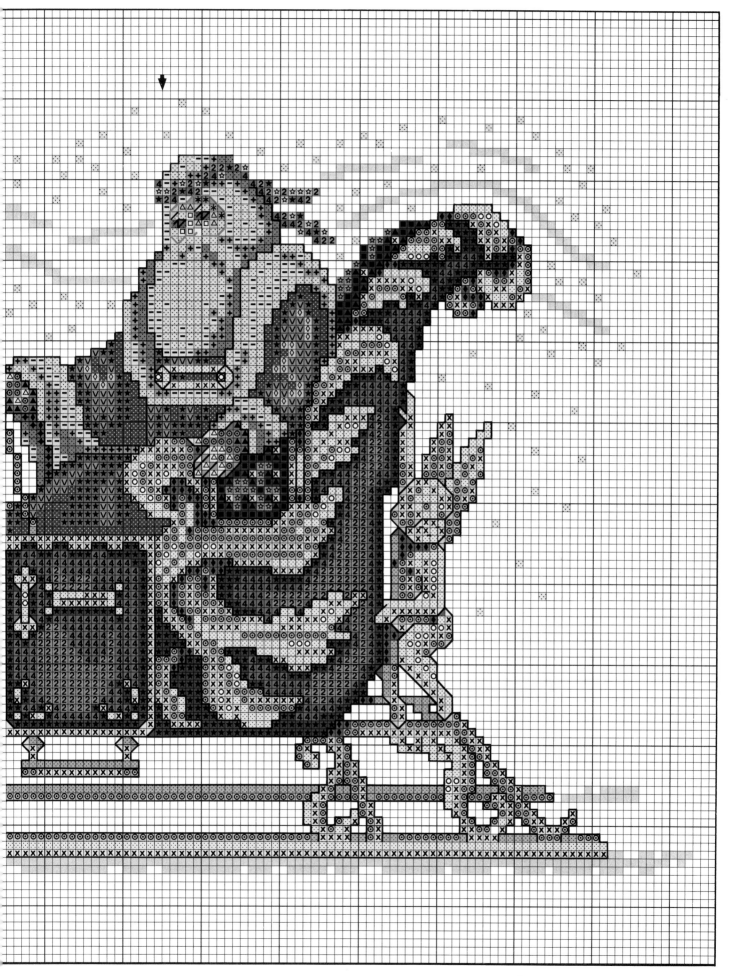

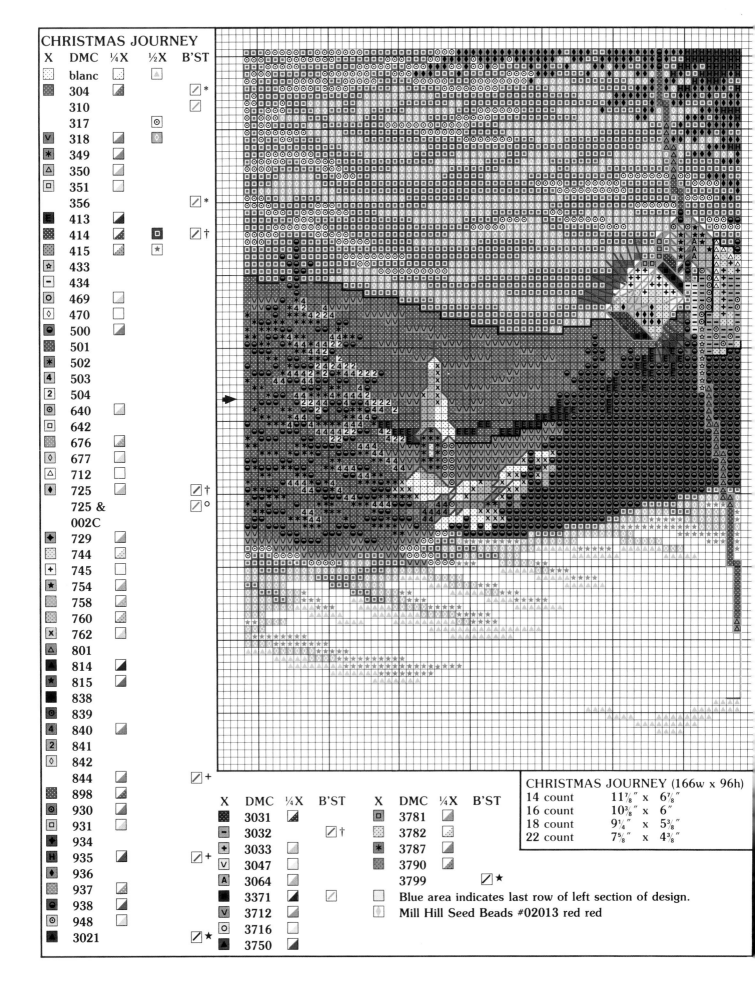

CHRISTMAS JOURNEY

X	DMC	¼X	½X	B'ST
	blanc			
	304			*
	310			
	317			
V	318			
*	349			
△	350			
□	351			
	356			*
	413			
	414			†
	415			
☆	433			
-	434			
⊙	469			
◇	470			
◉	500			
*	501			
*	502			
4	503			
2	504			
⊙	640			
□	642			
	676			
◇	677			
△	712			
◆	725			†
	725 & 002C			°
◆	729			
	744			
+	745			
★	754			
	758			
	760			
×	762			
△	801			
▲	814			
★	815			
■	838			
◉	839			
4	840			
2	841			
◇	842			
	844			+
	898			
◉	930			
□	931			
◆	934			
H	935			+
◆	936			
	937			
◉	938			
⊙	948			
▲	3021			★

X	DMC	¼X	B'ST		X	DMC	¼X	B'ST
	3031				□	3781		
-	3032		†			3782		
+	3033				*	3787		
V	3047					3790		
A	3064					3799		★
■	3371							
V	3712							
⊙	3716							
▲	3750							

Blue area indicates last row of left section of design.

Mill Hill Seed Beads #02013 red red

CHRISTMAS JOURNEY (166w x 96h)

14 count	11⅞"	x	6⅞"
16 count	10⅜"	x	6"
18 count	9¼"	x	5⅜"
22 count	7⅝"	x	4⅜"

* DMC 304 for drum. DMC 356 for hands and face.
† DMC 414 for shadows in snow. Use **2** strands DMC 725 for windows and **1** strand for lantern. DMC 3032 for eyebrows, hair, and beard.
+ DMC 844 for buildings. DMC 935 for holly leaves.
★ DMC 3021 for fur trim. DMC 3799 for mountains.
○ Use **1** strand of floss and **1** strand of Kreinik Cord Blending Filament #002C gold.

Christmas Journey (shown on pages 14-15): The design was stitched over two fabric threads on a 22″ x 16″ piece of Antique White Lugana (25 ct). Three strands of floss were used for Cross Stitch and 1 for Half Cross Stitch and Backstitch (unless otherwise indicated in color key). It was custom framed.

Needlework adaptation by Nancy Dockter.

OLDE SANTA (68w x 100h)

X	DMC	¼X	B'ST	ANC.	COLOR
⊞	blanc	⊡		2	white
■	310	◩	◹	403	black
▲	312	◪		979	dk blue
▽	318	◪		399	grey
=	321	◪	◹	9046	red
⊞	415	⊡		398	lt grey
⊙	420			374	dk beige
◇	422	◻		373	lt beige
◕	433	◪		358	dk tan
◆	435			1046	tan
△	437	◪		362	lt tan
✳	498	◪		1005	dk red
▼	645			273	dk taupe
	646		◹	8581	taupe
◉	647		◹	1040	lt taupe
▢	648			900	vy lt taupe
✳	676	◻		891	lt gold
✦	680			901	dk gold
◒	699	◪		923	dk green
○	703	◪		238	lt green
−	712	◻		926	cream
▦	729	◪	◹	890	gold
☆	739	◪		387	vy lt tan
▢	744	◪		301	yellow
◉	761	◪		1021	pink
◇	775	◻		128	vy lt blue
★	806			169	blue
⬠	807			168	lt blue
✦	814	◪		45	plum
▦	815			43	vy dk red
▲	839			360	dk brown
▦	840	◪		379	brown
★	841			378	lt brown
=	842	◻		388	vy lt brown
▦*	844			1041	dk grey
◆	911	◪		205	green
▼	946	◪		332	orange
▢	948	◻		1011	flesh
+	963	◻		73	lt pink
▦	3045			888	beige
✕	3072	◪		847	blue green
+	3078	◻		292	lt yellow
●	310		black French Knot		
●	321		red French Knot		
●	729		gold French Knot		

* For Santa's eyes, work an **x**, then a **+**.

Olde Santa (shown on page 17): The design was stitched over two fabric threads on a 14" x 16" piece of Cream Lugana (25 ct). Three strands of floss were used for Cross Stitch and 1 for Backstitch and French Knots. It was custom framed.

The design was also stitched over two fabric threads on a 14" x 16" piece of Raw Dublin Linen (25 ct). Three strands of floss were used for Cross Stitch and 1 for Backstitch and French Knots. It was custom framed.

Design adapted from a Family Line, Inc. greeting card.
Original artwork by Peggy Jo Ackley.

OLDE SANTA (68w x 100h)

Aida 11	6¼"	x 9⅛"
Aida 14	4⅞"	x 7¼"
Aida 18	3⅞"	x 5⅝"
Hardanger 22	3⅛"	x 4⅝"

Come rain or snow, our classic All-Weather Santa (shown custom framed on page 26) *won't be kept from his rounds. Here, the turn-of-the century fellow is stitched without his umbrella and displayed in a wall planter.*

ALL-WEATHER SANTA (69w x 117h)

X	DMC	¼X	½X	B'ST	COLOR
	blanc				white
	310			✓	black
V	320	◩			green
✚	321	◩			lt red
4	347	◩			rose
C	420			✓	vy dk gold
	498				red
	640		◼	✓	dk beige
◔	642				beige
S	644	◩			lt beige
✦	676	◻			lt gold
◆	680				dk gold
2	729	◩			gold
	754	◻			lt peach
▲	758	◩			peach
✳	814				dk red
−	822	◻			vy lt beige
	839			✓	brown
◻	924				vy dk blue
B	926	◩			blue
O	927				lt blue
◇	928				vy lt blue
8	962				pink
5	3021				vy dk grey
A	3022				grey
R	3023				lt grey
N	3024				vy lt grey
	3064	◩			dk peach
E	3328				lt rose
★	3768	◩			dk blue
◉	3787				dk grey
◬	3790	◩			vy dk beige
	gold metallic			✓	
•	310				black French Knot

All-Weather Santa (shown on page 26): The design was stitched over two fabric threads on a 14" x 19" piece of Cream Lugana (25 ct). Three strands of floss were used for Cross Stitch, 1 for Half Cross Stitch, 3 for gold metallic Backstitch, 1 for all other Backstitch, and 1 for French Knots. It was custom framed.

The design (shown on facing page) was also stitched, omitting umbrella, over two fabric threads on a 10" x 18" piece of Tea-Dyed Irish Linen (28 ct). Umbrella handle was replaced with coat colors and snowflakes were randomly added in place of umbrella (refer to photo for placement). Three strands of floss were used for Cross Stitch, 1 for Half Cross Stitch, 3 for gold metallic Backstitch, 1 for all other Backstitch, and 1 for French Knots. It was inserted in a planter frame.

Design by Carol Emmer.

ALL-WEATHER SANTA (69w x 117h)		
Aida 11	6⅜"	x 10¾"
Aida 14	5"	x 8⅜"
Aida 18	3⅞"	x 6½"
Hardanger 22	3¼"	x 5⅜"

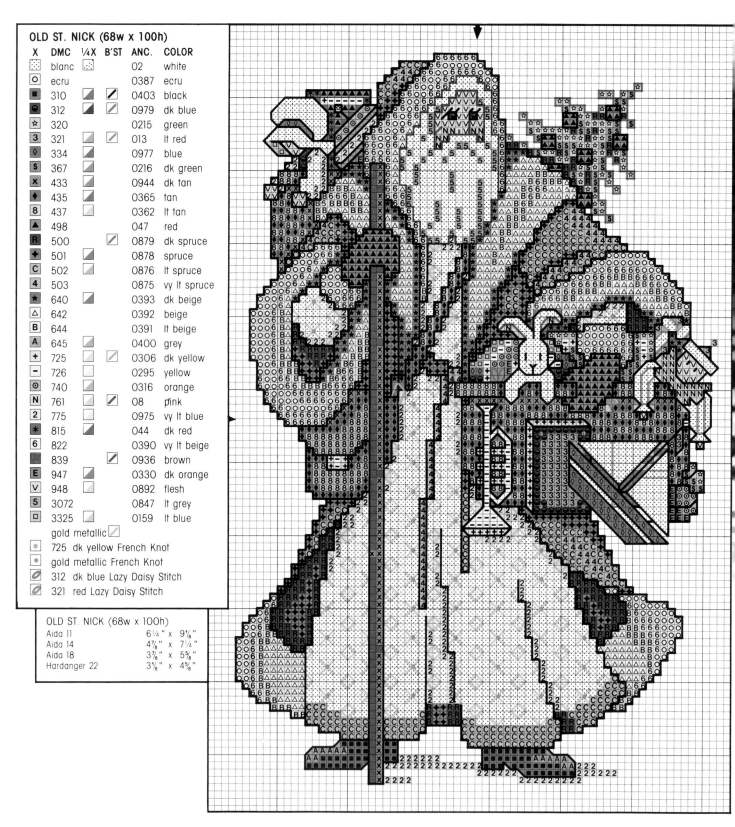

OLD ST. NICK (68w x 100h)

X	DMC	1/4X	B'ST	ANC.	COLOR
▦	blanc	▦		02	white
O	ecru			0387	ecru
■	310	◢	◥	0403	black
◕	312	◢	◥	0979	dk blue
☆	320			0215	green
3	321	◢	◥	013	lt red
◇	334	◢		0977	blue
S	367	◢		0216	dk green
X	433	◢		0944	dk tan
◆	435	◢		0365	tan
8	437	◢		0362	lt tan
▲	498			047	red
R	500		◥	0879	dk spruce
◆	501	◢		0878	spruce
C	502	◢		0876	lt spruce
4	503			0875	vy lt spruce
★	640	◢		0393	dk beige
△	642			0392	beige
B	644			0391	lt beige
A	645	◢		0400	grey
+	725	◢	◥	0306	dk yellow
–	726	◢		0295	yellow
◉	740			0316	orange
N	761	◢	◥	08	pink
2	775	◢		0975	vy lt blue
✳	815	◢		044	dk red
6	822			0390	vy lt beige
▨	839		◥	0936	brown
E	947	◢		0330	dk orange
V	948	◢		0892	flesh
5	3072			0847	lt grey
▢	3325	◢		0159	lt blue
	gold metallic	◥			
◦	725 dk yellow French Knot				
◦	gold metallic French Knot				
⊘	312 dk blue Lazy Daisy Stitch				
⊘	321 red Lazy Daisy Stitch				

OLD ST. NICK (68w x 100h)

Aida 11	6¼" x 9⅛"
Aida 14	4⅞" x 7¼"
Aida 18	3⅞" x 5⅝"
Hardanger 22	3⅛" x 4⅝"

Old St. Nick (shown on page 18): The design was stitched over two fabric threads on a 14" x 16" piece of Cream Lugana (25 ct). Three strands of floss were used for Cross Stitch, 1 for Backstitch, 1 for French Knots, and 1 for Lazy Daisy Stitches. It was custom framed.

The design (shown on page 19) was also stitched on a 1¼ yd piece of Cracked Wheat Ragusa (14 ct). It was made into an afghan.
For afghan, cut off selvages of fabric.

(**Note**: Fabric should measure 45" x 55".) To make fringe, measure 5" from one raw edge of fabric and pull out one fabric thread. Unravel fabric up to missing thread. Repeat for each side. Tie an overhand knot at each corner with 4 horizontal and 4 vertical fabric threads. Working from corners, use 8 fabric threads for each knot until all threads are knotted. Folding corners at an angle, pin 4 yards of ⅞"w reversible grosgrain ribbon 4½" from fringe on all sides of fabric. Overlap ends of ribbon and turn under ½" of top ribbon; baste ribbon to fabric. Machine stitch along each edge of ribbon. To mark design placement, tie a piece of thread to fabric 9" from bottom ribbon and 7" from right side ribbon. Match center of design to piece of thread tied on fabric. Stitching over 2 threads, use 6 strands of floss for Cross Stitch, 2 for Backstitch, 2 for French Knots, and 2 for Lazy Daisy Stitches.

Design by Terrie Lee Steinmeyer.

FATHER CHRISTMAS (59w x 104h)

X	DMC	¼X	B'ST	ANC.	COLOR
▨	blanc	▨		02	white
O	ecru	▫		0387	ecru
X	223		▱	0895	rose
⊙	224	▫		0893	lt rose
■	310	◪	▱	0403	black
−	353	◪		08	dk peach
▢	407		▱	0882	tan
★	520		▱	0862	dk green
5	522			0860	green
◇	524			0858	lt green
*	543	▫		0933	lt beige
▲	646			8581	dk grey
+	648	◪		0900	grey
☆	754			4146	peach
△	760	◪		09	vy dk peach
S	819	◪		048	lt pink
■	838	◪		0380	dk brown
H	839	◪	▱	0936	brown
V	840			0379	lt brown
◆	841		▱	0378	dk beige
B	842	◪		0376	beige
C	844	◪		0401	vy dk grey
N	926			0850	blue
3	948			0892	lt peach
▫	950	▫		0881	lt tan
◕	962			027	vy dk pink
▨	963			024	pink
4	3064	◪		0914	dk tan
2	3072	◪		0847	lt grey
6	3326	◪		025	dk pink
•	ecru French Knot				
•	842 beige French Knot				

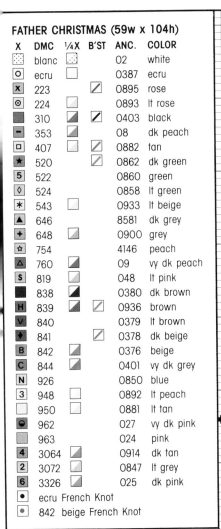

Father Christmas (shown on page 22): The design was stitched over two fabric threads on a 13" x 17" piece of Cream Lugana (25 ct). Three strands of floss were used for Cross Stitch, 1 for Backstitch, and 1 for French Knots. It was custom framed.

The design (shown on page 16) was also stitched over two fabric threads on a 10" x 14" piece of Cream Lugana (25 ct). Three strands of floss were used for Cross Stitch, 1 for Backstitch, and 1 for French Knots. It was applied to a tree skirt.

For tree skirt top, fold a 45" square of fabric in half from top to bottom and again from left to right. To mark outer cutting line, tie one end of a 25" length of string to a fabric marking pen. Insert a thumbtack through string 21½" from pen. Insert thumbtack in fabric as shown in **Fig. 1** and mark one-fourth of a circle.

Fig. 1

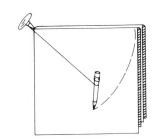

FATHER CHRISTMAS (59w x 104h)	
Aida 11	5⅜" x 9½"
Aida 14	4¼" x 7½"
Aida 18	3⅜" x 5⅞"
Hardanger 22	2¾" x 4¾"

Inserting thumbtack through string 3" from pen, repeat to mark a 6" dia. inner cutting line. Following cutting lines and cutting through all thicknesses, cut out skirt. For slit in back of skirt, cut along one fold from outer edge to inner edge.

For tree skirt backing, cut a piece of fabric and a piece of batting same size as tree skirt top. Baste batting to wrong side of backing fabric along edges.

Continued on page 141.

Note: For our tree skirt, we stitched **Olde Santa** (page 83) and **Old St. Nick** (page 86) on Cream Lugana (over 2 threads) and placed one on each side of **Father Christmas**.

Design by Carol Emmer.

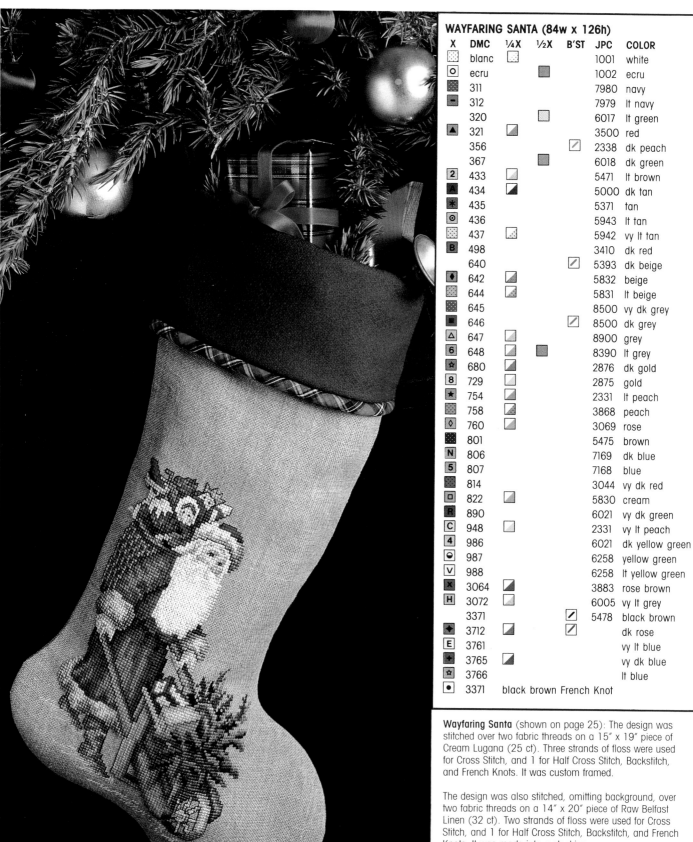

WAYFARING SANTA (84w x 126h)

X	DMC	1/4X	1/2X	B'ST	JPC	COLOR
▦	blanc	▦			1001	white
O	ecru		▦		1002	ecru
▦	311				7980	navy
▬	312				7979	lt navy
	320		▦		6017	lt green
▲	321	◹			3500	red
	356			◹	2338	dk peach
	367		▦		6018	dk green
2	433	◹			5471	lt brown
A	434	◥			5000	dk tan
✳	435				5371	tan
⊙	436				5943	lt tan
▦	437	▦			5942	vy lt tan
B	498				3410	dk red
	640			◹	5393	dk beige
◆	642	◹			5832	beige
▦	644	◹			5831	lt beige
	645				8500	vy dk grey
■	646			◹	8500	dk grey
△	647	◹			8900	grey
6	648	◹	▦		8390	lt grey
☆	680	◥			2876	dk gold
8	729	◹			2875	gold
★	754	◹			2331	lt peach
▦	758	◹			3868	peach
◊	760	◹			3069	rose
▦	801				5475	brown
N	806				7169	dk blue
5	807				7168	blue
▦	814				3044	vy dk red
□	822	◹			5830	cream
R	890				6021	vy dk green
C	948	◹			2331	vy lt peach
4	986				6021	dk yellow green
⊙	987				6258	yellow green
V	988	◥			6258	lt yellow green
✕	3064	◥			3883	rose brown
H	3072	◹			6005	vy lt grey
	3371			◹	5478	black brown
◆	3712	◥		◹		dk rose
E	3761					vy lt blue
✦	3765	◥				vy dk blue
☆	3766					lt blue
●	3371	black brown French Knot				

Wayfaring Santa (shown on page 25): The design was stitched over two fabric threads on a 15" x 19" piece of Cream Lugana (25 ct). Three strands of floss were used for Cross Stitch, and 1 for Half Cross Stitch, Backstitch, and French Knots. It was custom framed.

The design was also stitched, omitting background, over two fabric threads on a 14" x 20" piece of Raw Belfast Linen (32 ct). Two strands of floss were used for Cross Stitch, and 1 for Half Cross Stitch, Backstitch, and French Knots. It was made into a stocking.

For stocking, cut one 14" x 20" piece of Raw Belfast Linen for backing. Cut two 14" x 20" pieces of off-white fabric for lining. Cut two 4¼" x 14½" pieces of coordinating fabric for cuff. Continued on page 142.

WAYFARING SANTA (84w x 126h)

14 count	6"	x	9"
16 count	5¼"	x	7⅞"
18 count	4¾"	x	7"
22 count	3⅞"	x	5¾"

Kris Kringle (shown custom framed on page 23) *looks striking finished on a midnight black Anne Cloth afghan.*

KRIS KRINGLE (66w x 108h)

X	DMC	¼X	¾X	B'ST	COLOR
	blanc				white
	310			✓	black
▲	420				dk golden brown
▬	433				lt brown
✕	500		◩		dk green
▽	642			✓	beige grey
▢	644		◩		lt beige grey
★	676			✓	lt golden brown
☆	712				vy lt beige
C	729				golden brown
	754	◩			lt flesh
◇	758		◩		dk flesh
▬	760		◩		dk pink
	761		◩		pink
◉	801		◩		brown
▬	822		◩		vy lt beige grey
	869		◩		vy dk golden brown
	898		◩		dk brown
▽	905		◩		dk yellow green
△	906				yellow green
✳	907				lt yellow green
●	938				vy dk brown
○	948				vy lt flesh
◉	986				green
	3021			✓	vy dk beige
◒	3033				lt beige
	3371			✓	brown black
C	3778		◩		vy dk flesh
▦	3779		◩		flesh
◆	3781		◩		dk beige
✚	3782				beige
▦	3790		◩		✓	dk beige grey

KRIS KRINGLE (66w x 108h)

14 count	4¾" x 7¾"
16 count	4⅛" x 6¾"
18 count	3¾" x 6"
22 count	3" x 5"

Kris Kringle (shown on page 23): The design was stitched over two fabric threads on a 14" x 17" piece of Cream Lugana (25 ct). Three strands of floss were used for Cross Stitch, 2 for lt golden brown Backstitch, and 1 for all other Backstitch. It was custom framed.

The design (shown on facing page) was also stitched over two fabric threads on a 45" x 58" piece (standard afghan size) of Midnight Black Anne Cloth (18 ct). It was made into an afghan.

For afghan, cut off selvages of fabric; measure 5½" from raw edge of fabric and pull out one fabric thread. Fringe fabric up to missing thread. Repeat for each side. Tie an overhand knot at each corner with 4 horizontal and 4 vertical fabric threads. Working from corners, use 8 fabric threads for each knot until all threads are knotted.

Refer to Diagram for placement of design on fabric. Six strands of floss were used for Cross Stitch, 3 for lt golden brown Backstitch, and 2 for all other Backstitch.

DIAGRAM

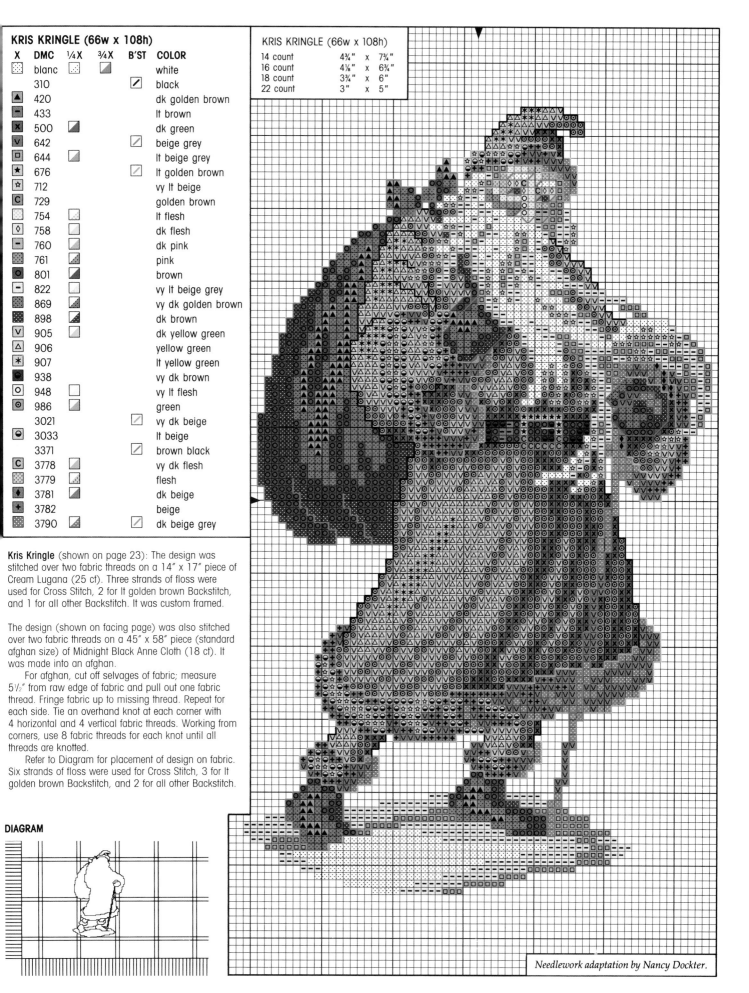

Needlework adaptation by Nancy Dockter.

ROOFTOP ST. NICK (73w x 114h)

X	DMC	1/4X	1/2X	B'ST	JPC	COLOR
	blanc				1001	white
O	320				6017	green
	349				2335	red orange
♦	356				2338	vy dk peach
▬	367				6018	dk green
✳	368				6016	lt green
C	433				5471	brown
★	434				5000	lt brown
□	436				5943	vy lt brown
⊖	498				3410	red
▲	610				5889	dk tan
	611				5898	tan
4	612					lt tan
	613					vy lt tan
	640				5393	dk beige

X	DMC	1/4X	JPC	COLOR
	642		5832	beige
⊙	644		5831	lt beige
✦	645		8500	dk grey
△	646		8500	grey
▬	647		8900	lt grey
	676		2874	gold
S	677			lt gold
★	680		2876	vy dk gold
O	729		2875	dk gold
	754		2331	lt peach
◇	758		3868	peach
4	801		5475	dk brown
✳	815		3000	vy dk red
	816		3410	dk red
X	817		2335	dk red orange

X	DMC	1/4X	3/4X	B'ST	JPC	COLOR
8	822				5830	vy lt beige
2	844				8501	vy dk grey
⊡	918				3340	rust
	931				7051	blue
▨	938				5477	vy dk brown
+	948				2331	vy lt peach
	3031				5472	grey brown
-	3064				3883	flesh
	3371				5478	brown black
S	3706				3127	dk pink
☆	3708				3127	pink
	3721					rose
V	3772				5579	dk flesh
3	3778					dk peach
●	816					dk red French Knot

Rooftop St. Nick (shown on page 27): The design was stitched over two fabric threads on a 14" x 18" piece of Cream Lugana (25 ct). Three strands of floss were used for Cross Stitch, 2 for French Knots, and 1 for Half Cross Stitch and Backstitch. It was custom framed.

The design was also stitched over two fabric threads on a 14" x 18" piece of Tea-Dyed Irish Linen (28 ct). Three strands of floss were used for Cross Stitch, 2 for French Knots, and 1 for Half Cross Stitch and Backstitch. It was made into a pillow.

For pillow, center design and trim stitched piece to measure 7³/₄" x 11³/₄". Cut a piece of fabric the same size as stitched piece for lining. Baste lining fabric to back of stitched piece close to raw edges.

Cut two 11³/₄" lengths of purchased gold metallic cording with attached seam allowance. If needed, trim seam allowance to ¹/₂". Matching raw edges, baste one length of cording to right side of each long side of stitched piece. Press seam allowances toward stitched piece.

For pillow front and back, cut two 16³/₄" x 11³/₄" pieces of fabric. Center stitched piece right side up on the right side of one piece of fabric; pin in place. Using zipper foot and same color thread as cording, attach stitched piece to pillow front by sewing as close as possible to cording, taking care not to catch fabric of stitched piece.

For fabric cording, cut one 65" x 2¹/₂" bias strip of fabric. Center purchased cord on wrong side of bias strip; matching long edges, fold strip over cord. Using zipper foot, baste along length of strip close to cord; trim seam allowance to ¹/₂".

Matching raw edges and beginning at bottom center, pin cording to right side of pillow front making a ³/₈" clip in seam allowance of cording at each corner. Ends of cording should overlap approx. 2"; pin overlapping end out of the way. Starting 2" from beginning end of cording and ending 4" from overlapping end, baste cording to pillow front. On overlapping end of cording, remove 2¹/₂" of basting; fold end of fabric back and trim cord so that it meets beginning end of cord. Fold end of fabric under ¹/₂"; wrap fabric over beginning end of cording. Finish basting cording to pillow front.

Matching right sides and leaving an opening for turning, use a ¹/₂" seam allowance to sew pillow front and backing fabric together. Trim corners diagonally. Turn pillow right side out, carefully pushing corners outward. Stuff pillow with polyester fiberfill and sew final closure by hand.

Needlework adaptation by Carol Emmer.

ROOFTOP ST. NICK (73w x 114h)

count			
14 count	5¼"	x	8¼"
16 count	4⅝"	x	7⅛"
18 count	4⅛"	x	6⅜"
22 count	3⅜"	x	5¼"

STITCH COUNT (49w x 102h)

Count		
14 count	3½" x	7⅜"
16 count	3⅛" x	6⅜"
18 count	2¾" x	5¾"
22 count	2¼" x	4¾"

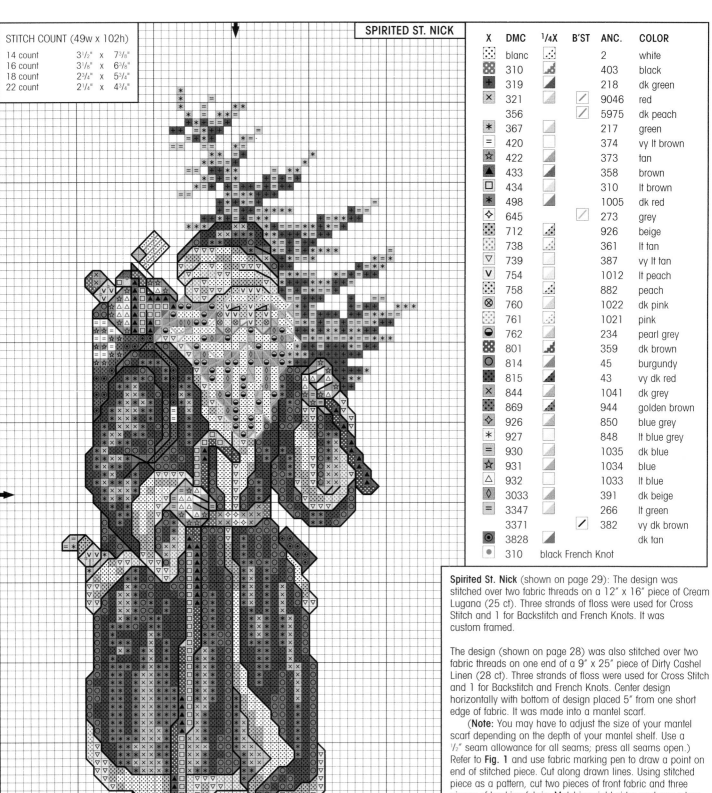

X	DMC	¼X	B'ST	ANC.	COLOR
∷	blanc	∷		2	white
▓	310	◣		403	black
✚	319	◥		218	dk green
✕	321	◥	╱	9046	red
	356		╱	5975	dk peach
✱	367	◥		217	green
=	420			374	vy lt brown
☆	422	◥		373	tan
▲	433	◥		358	brown
▢	434	◥		310	lt brown
✻	498	◥		1005	dk red
◇	645	◢	╱	273	grey
⬚	712	◢		926	beige
⬚	738	◢		361	lt tan
▽	739			387	vy lt tan
∨	754	◥		1012	lt peach
⬚	758	◢		882	peach
⊗	760	◥		1022	dk pink
⬚	761	∷		1021	pink
◒	762	◥		234	pearl grey
▓	801	◢		359	dk brown
○	814	◥		45	burgundy
▦	815	◥		43	vy dk red
✕	844	◥		1041	dk grey
⬚	869	◢		944	golden brown
◈	926	◥		850	blue grey
✳	927			848	lt blue grey
=	930	◥		1035	dk blue
☆	931	◥		1034	blue
△	932			1033	lt blue
◇	3033	◥		391	dk beige
=	3347	◥		266	lt green
	3371		╱	382	vy dk brown
◉	3828	◥			dk tan
●	310				black French Knot

Spirited St. Nick (shown on page 29): The design was stitched over two fabric threads on a 12" x 16" piece of Cream Lugana (25 ct). Three strands of floss were used for Cross Stitch and 1 for Backstitch and French Knots. It was custom framed.

The design (shown on page 28) was also stitched over two fabric threads on one end of a 9" x 25" piece of Dirty Cashel Linen (28 ct). Three strands of floss were used for Cross Stitch and 1 for Backstitch and French Knots. Center design horizontally with bottom of design placed 5" from one short edge of fabric. It was made into a mantel scarf.

 (**Note:** You may have to adjust the size of your mantel scarf depending on the depth of your mantel shelf. Use a ½" seam allowance for all seams; press all seams open.) Refer to **Fig. 1** and use fabric marking pen to draw a point on end of stitched piece. Cut along drawn lines. Using stitched piece as a pattern, cut two pieces of front fabric and three pieces of backing fabric. Matching right sides and raw edges, sew one front piece to stitched piece along long side edge only. Repeat using remaining front piece and long side edge of stitched piece. For back, repeat using three backing pieces. Matching right sides and raw edges and leaving an opening for turning, sew front to back. Clip corners; turn right side out. Blind stitch opening closed. Hand sew a purchased 3" tassel to each point.

Needlework adaptation by Jane Chandler.

Fig. 1

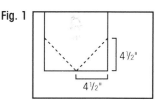

4½"

4½"

SANTA IN BLUE (65w x 102h)

X	DMC	¼X	B'ST	ANC.	COLOR
	blanc			02	white
	309			042	lt rose
	310		✓	0403	black
	319			0218	dk green
	320			0216	lt green
	326			059	rose
	336			0149	dk blue
	341			0117	vy lt blue
	367			0217	green
	368			0215	vy lt green
	433			0371	brown
	434			0310	lt brown
	435			0365	vy dk tan
	436			0363	dk tan
	437			0362	tan
	498			043	dk rose
	640		✓	0393	dk beige
	642			0392	beige
	644			0391	lt beige
	645			0400	dk grey
	646			8581	grey
	647			0900	lt grey
	648			0398	vy lt grey
	738			0367	lt tan
	739			0366	vy lt tan
	754			4146	lt flesh
	758		✓	0882	flesh
	760			0894	coral
	761			0893	lt coral
	780			0309	vy dk gold
	781			0308	dk gold
	782			0307	gold
	783			0306	lt gold
	792			0941	blue
	793		✓	0121	lt blue
	815			044	red
	818			048	vy lt pink
	822			0387	vy lt beige
	839		✓	0936	dk brown
	844			0401	vy dk grey
	899			027	dk pink
	902			072	maroon
	962		✓	076	pink
	3064			0914	dk flesh
	3326			026	lt pink
	copper metallic	✓			
	793				lt blue French Knot

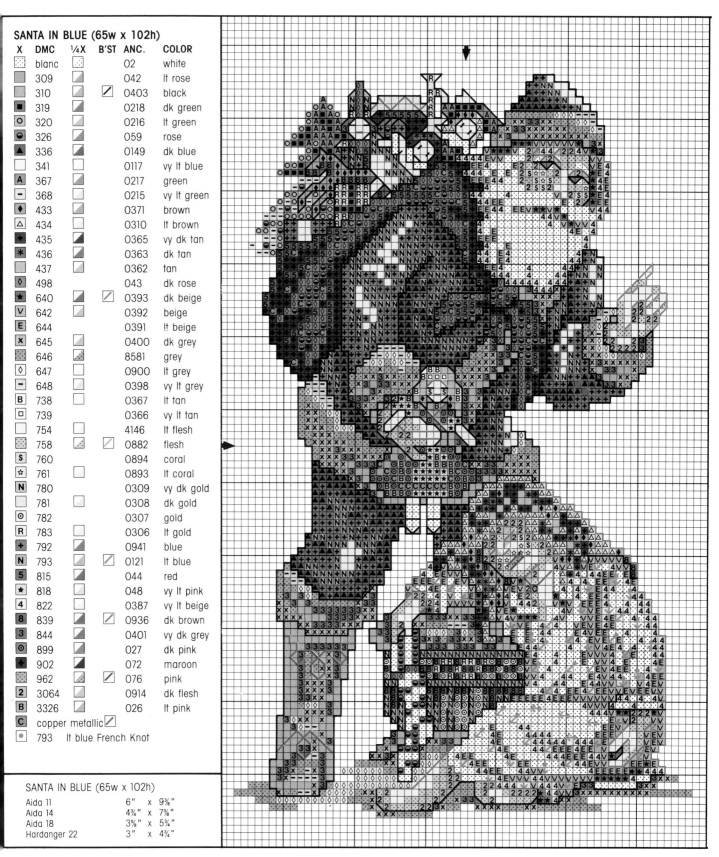

SANTA IN BLUE (65w x 102h)

Aida 11	6"	x 9⅜"
Aida 14	4¾"	x 7⅜"
Aida 18	3⅝"	x 5¾"
Hardanger 22	3"	x 4¾"

Santa In Blue (shown on page 21): The design was stitched over two fabric threads on a 14" x 19" piece of Cream Lugana (25 ct). Three strands of floss were used for Cross Stitch and 1 for Backstitch and French Knots. It was custom framed.

The design (shown on page 20) was also stitched over two fabric threads on a 13" x 17" piece of Raw Belfast Linen (32 ct) with center of design 6¼" from left (13") edge and 8¼" from bottom edge of fabric. Two strands of floss were used for

Cross Stitch and 1 for Backstitch and French Knots. It was made into a stocking. Continued on page 142.

Design by Carol Emmer

Our gentlemanly Santa (shown custom framed on page 24) *is stitched on rustic fabric for a Yuletide wall hanging.*

SANTA'S JOURNEY (77w x 102h)

X	DMC	¼X	½X	B'ST	ANC.	COLOR
	blanc		⊙		2	white
O	ecru				387	ecru
✤	319				218	dk green
◊	322				978	lt blue
−	347	◩		◿	1025	red
✱	350				11	lt red
8	353				6	pink
	356			◿	5975	vy dk peach
	434	◩		◿	310	tan

X	DMC	¼X	B'ST	ANC.	COLOR
⊖	436			1045	lt tan
▣	500			683	vy dk green
▦	646	◩	◿	8581	grey
✖	648			900	lt grey
V	676			891	lt gold
◆	680		◿	901	dk gold
⊙	729			890	gold
N	754		◿	1012	lt peach
	758		◿	882	peach

X	DMC	¼X	½X	B'ST	ANC.	COLOR
▦	760	◩			1022	rose
H	801		◿		359	brown
2	816				1005	dk red
▦	*823 &		◿			
	930					
⊙	*829 &					
	3031					
▪	831				277	olive
△	833				907	lt olive
✦	*905 &					
	904					
✳	906				256	yellow green
8	907				255	lt yellow green
☆	926		★		850	dk grey blue
4	927		⊙		848	grey blue
▦	930	◩			1035	blue
▢	934				862	grey green
▦	948	◩			1011	lt pink
✖	987		◆		244	green
	3031			◿	360	dk brown
◆	3064	◩			883	dk peach
⊙	3072				847	vy lt grey
N	3328				1024	vy dk rose
▦	*3345 &		◿			
	936					
★	3347		✕		266	lt green
H	3364		S		260	vy lt green
◼	3371	◩		◿	382	vy dk brown
▲	3712				1023	dk rose
	3799			◿	236	dk grey
•	3371			vy dk brown French Knot		
•	3799			dk grey French Knot		

* For framed piece, use 2 strands of first floss color listed and 1 strand of second floss color listed. For wall hanging, use 4 strands of first floss color listed and 2 strands of second floss color listed.

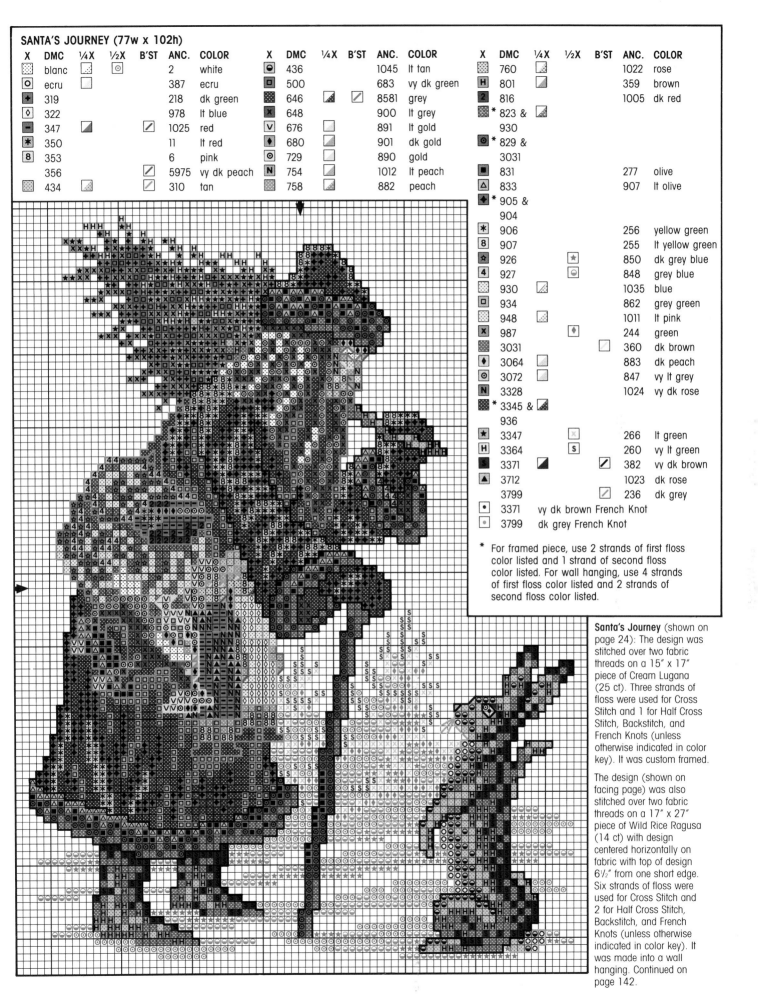

Santa's Journey (shown on page 24): The design was stitched over two fabric threads on a 15" x 17" piece of Cream Lugana (25 ct). Three strands of floss were used for Cross Stitch and 1 for Half Cross Stitch, Backstitch, and French Knots (unless otherwise indicated in color key). It was custom framed.

The design (shown on facing page) was also stitched over two fabric threads on a 17" x 27" piece of Wild Rice Ragusa (14 ct) with design centered horizontally on fabric with top of design 6½" from one short edge. Six strands of floss were used for Cross Stitch and 2 for Half Cross Stitch, Backstitch, and French Knots (unless otherwise indicated in color key). It was made into a wall hanging. Continued on page 142.

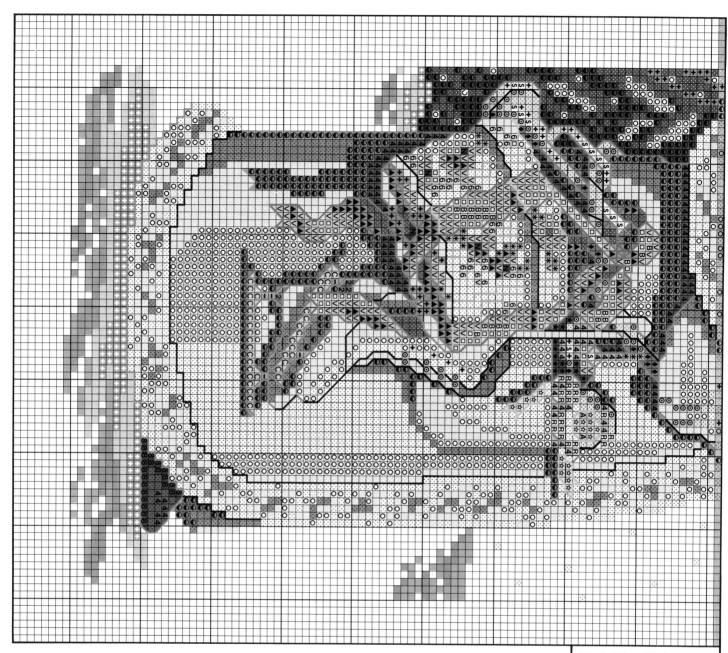

Santa (shown on page 31): The design was stitched over two fabric threads on a 13" x 21" piece of Tile Blue Linda (27 ct). Three strands of floss were used for Cross Stitch and 1 for Backstitch. It was custom framed.

The upper portion of Santa **only** (refer to photo on page 30) was also stitched over two fabric threads on an 8" x 15" piece of Tile Blue Linda (27 ct). Three strands of floss were used for Cross Stitch and 1 for Half Cross Stitch and Backstitch. It was made into a pillow.

For pillow, trim stitched piece 1 1/2" larger than design on all sides. Cut two 3 1/2" x 9 5/8" pieces of fabric for side panels. Cut one 12 3/4" x 9 5/8" piece of fabric for backing.

For cording, cut one 68" x 2 1/2" bias strip of fabric. Center purchased cord on wrong side of bias strip; matching long edges, fold strip over cord. Using zipper foot, baste along length of strip close to cord; trim seam allowance to 1/2".

For pillow top, cut two 9 5/8" lengths of cording. Matching raw edges, pin one length of cording to right side of each long side of stitched piece; sew cording to stitched piece. Matching right sides and raw edges, pin one side panel to each long side of stitched piece over cording; sew side panels to stitched piece.

Matching raw edges and beginning at bottom edge, pin remaining cording to right side of pillow top, making a 3/8" clip in seam allowance of cording at each corner. Ends of cording should overlap approx. 2"; pin overlapping end out of the way. Starting 2" from beginning end of cording and ending 4" from overlapping end, sew cording to stitched piece. On overlapping end of cording remove 2 1/2" of basting; fold end of fabric back and trim cord so it meets beginning end of cord. Fold end of fabric under 1/2"; wrap fabric over beginning end of cording. Finish sewing cording to pillow top.

Matching right sides and leaving an opening for turning, use a 1/2" seam allowance to sew pillow top and backing fabric together. Trim corners diagonally. Turn pillow right side out, carefully pushing corners outward. Stuff pillow with polyester fiberfill and sew final closure by hand.

Design by Sandi Gore Evans.

SANTA (73w x 187h)			
14 count	5 1/4"	x	13 3/8"
16 count	4 5/8"	x	11 3/4"
18 count	4 1/8"	x	10 1/2"
22 count	3 3/8"	x	8 1/2"

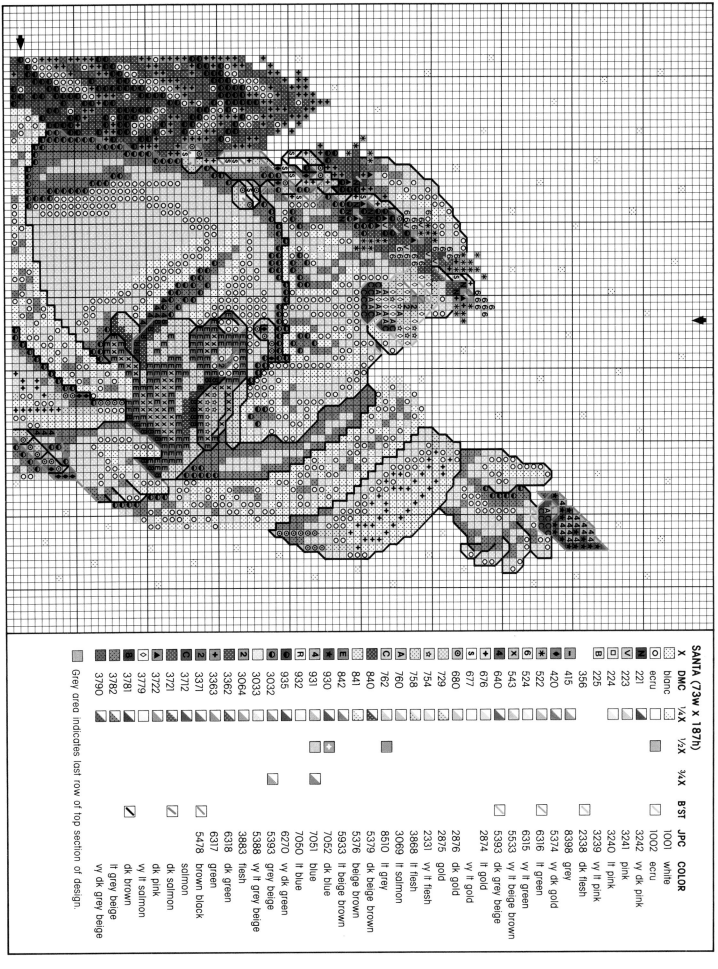

SANTA (73w x 187h)						
X	DMC	1/4X	1/2X	3/4X	B'ST	JPC	COLOR

	DMC					JPC	COLOR
X	blanc					1001	white
O	ecru					1002	ecru
V	223					3242	ecru
N	221					3241	pink
V	223					3240	lt pink
□	224					3239	vy lt pink
B	225					2338	vy lt pink
	356					5533	dk flesh
	415					8398	grey
	420					5374	vy dk gold
	422					6316	lt green
	524					6315	vy lt green
	543					5933	vy lt beige brown
	640					5393	dk grey beige
	543					2874	vy lt beige brown
	676					2876	lt gold
	677					2875	vy lt gold
	680					2876	dk gold
S	729					2331	gold
	754					2331	vy lt flesh
	758					3868	lt flesh
	760					3069	lt salmon
C	762					8510	lt grey
A	840					5379	dk grey
	841					5376	beige brown
E	842					5933	lt beige brown
R	930					7052	dk blue
4	931					7051	blue
	932					7050	lt blue
6	935					6270	vy dk green
C	3032					5393	grey beige
0	3033					5388	vy lt grey beige
2	3064					3883	flesh
2	3362					6318	dk green
C	3363					6317	green
2	3371					5478	brown black
C	3712					5478	salmon
	3721						dk salmon
B	3722						dk pink
	3779						vy lt salmon
B	3781						dk brown
B	3782						lt grey beige
	3790						vy dk grey beige

Grey area indicates last row of top section of design.

STRAIGHT TO HIS WORK (96w x 132h)

X	¼X	½X	B'ST	DMC	JPC	COLOR
				blanc	1001	white
				ecru	1002	ecru
				321	3500	red
				356	2338	dk peach
				420	5374	dk golden brown
				422	5372	lt golden brown
				498	3410	dk red
				500	6880	vy dk green
				501	6878	dk green
				502	6876	green
				503	6879	lt green
				504	6875	vy lt green
				610	5889	vy dk khaki
				611	5898	dk khaki
				612		khaki
				613		lt khaki
				642	5832	dk beige
				644	5831	beige
				666	3046	lt red
				676	2874	lt gold
				677		gold
				680	2876	vy dk gold

X	¼X	½X	B'ST	DMC	JPC	COLOR
				729	2875	dk gold
				741	2314	vy dk yellow
				743	2302	dk yellow
				744	2293	yellow
				745	2296	lt yellow
				754	2331	lt peach
				758	3868	peach
				814	3044	vy dk red
				822	5830	lt beige
				869		vy dk golden brown
				930	7052	vy dk blue
				931	7051	dk blue
				932	7050	blue
				962	3151	pink
				3031	5472	dk brown
				3045	2412	golden brown
				3371	5478	brown black
				3752	7876	lt blue
				3781		brown
				3371		brown black French Knot

Grey area indicates last row of top section of design.

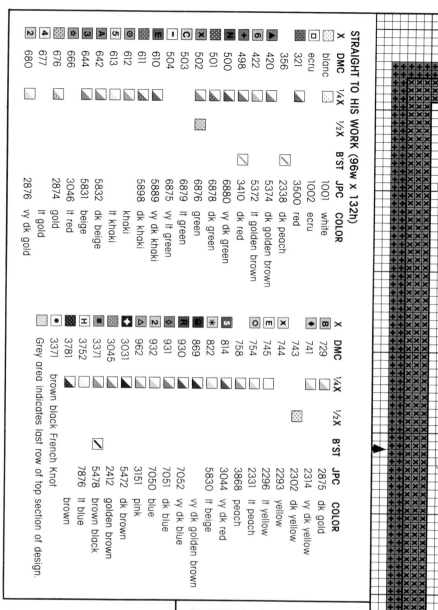

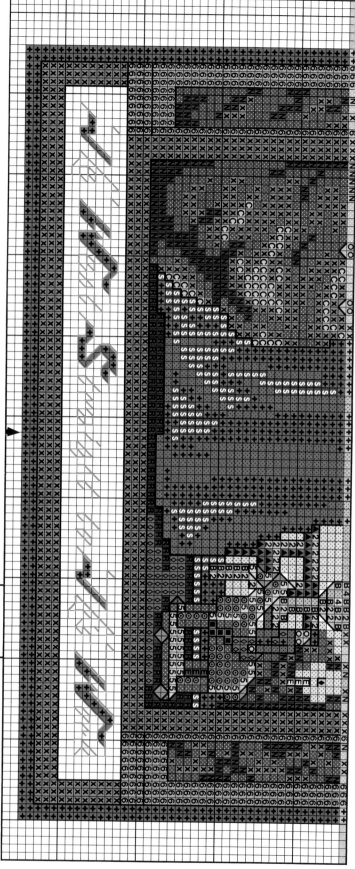

STRAIGHT TO HIS WORK (96w x 132h)

14 count	6⅞"	x	9½"
16 count	6"	x	8¼"
18 count	5⅜"	x	7⅜"
22 count	4⅜"	x	6"

Straight To His Work (shown on pages 32-33): The design was stitched over two fabric threads on a 16" x 19" piece of Khaki Linda (27 ct). Three strands of floss were used for Cross Stitch and 1 for Half Cross Stitch, Backstitch, and French Knots. It was custom framed.

Design by Marilyn Gandré.

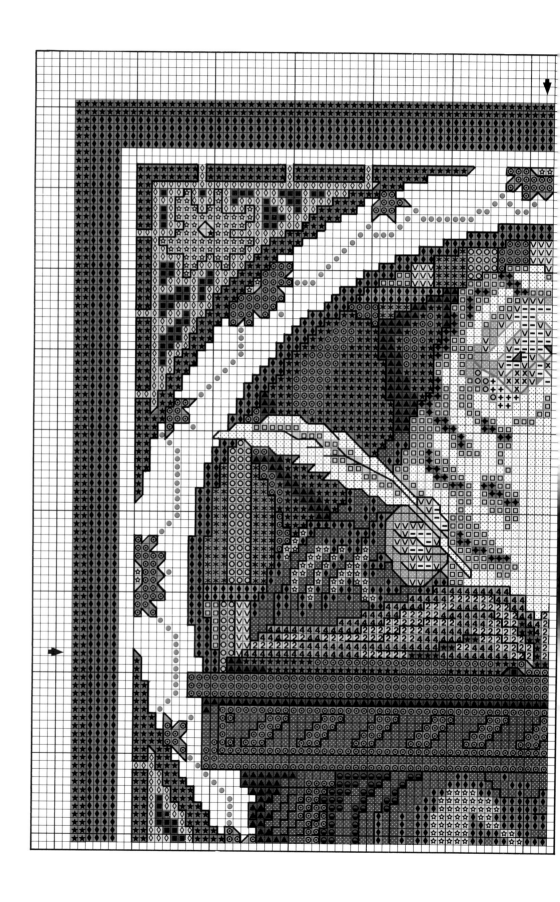

103

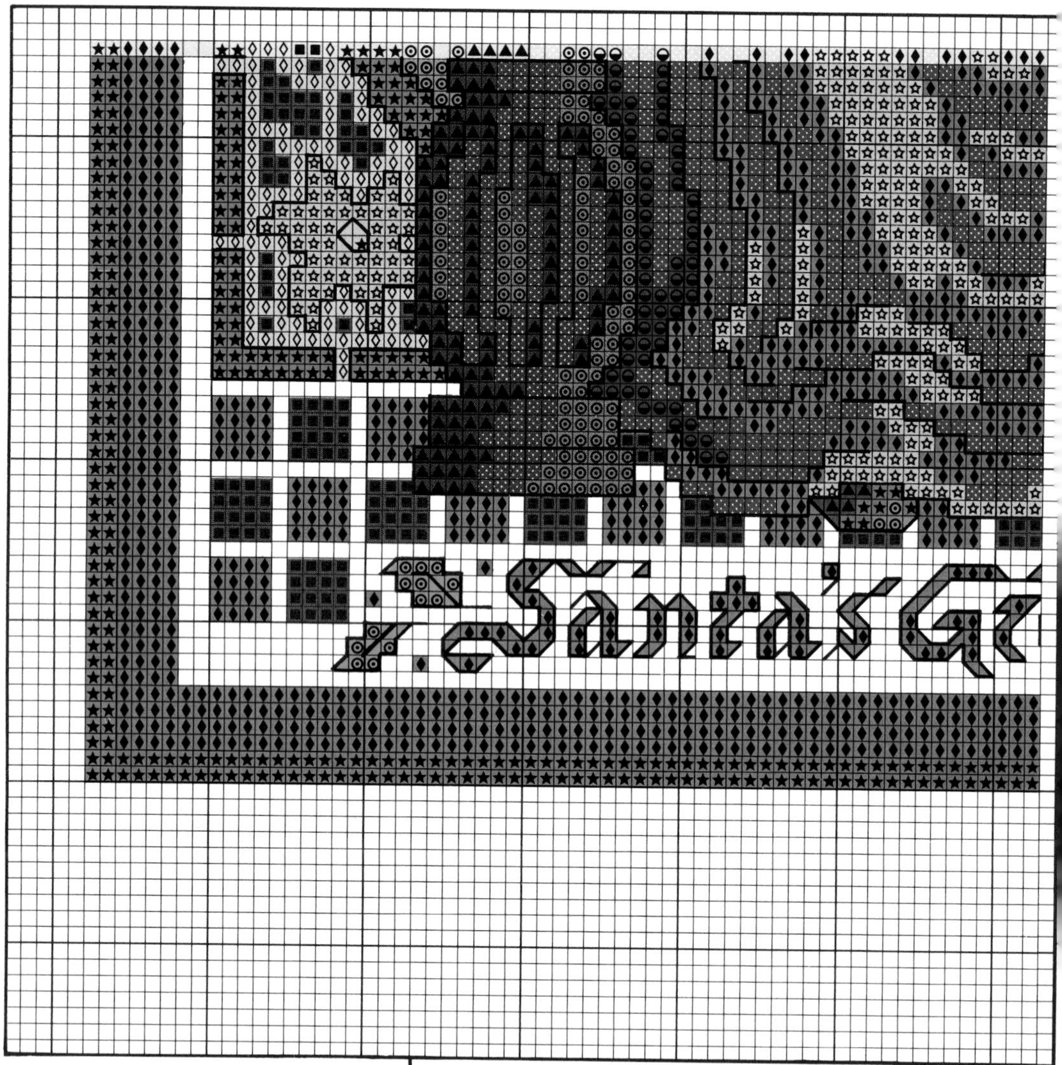

Santa's Great Book (shown on page 34): The design was stitched over two fabric threads on an 18" x 19" piece of Ivory Lugana (25 ct). Three strands of floss were used for Cross Stitch and 1 for Half Cross Stitch and Backstitch. It was custom framed.

Design by Marilyn Gandré.

SANTA'S GREAT BOOK (120w x 137h)

X	DMC	¼X	½X	B'ST	JPC	COLOR
⁘	blanc	□			1001	white
△	304				3401	red
■	310	□		□	8403	black
★	319	□			6246	green
☆	321	□			3500	lt red
○	335				3283	pink
♦	347				3013	salmon
◎	367	□			6018	lt green
⁘	407	□				dk flesh
	445		□		2288	yellow
✳	451				8233	grey
♦	498	□			3410	dk red
◇	503	□			6879	vy lt green
	640			□	5393	dk beige grey
♦	642				5832	beige grey

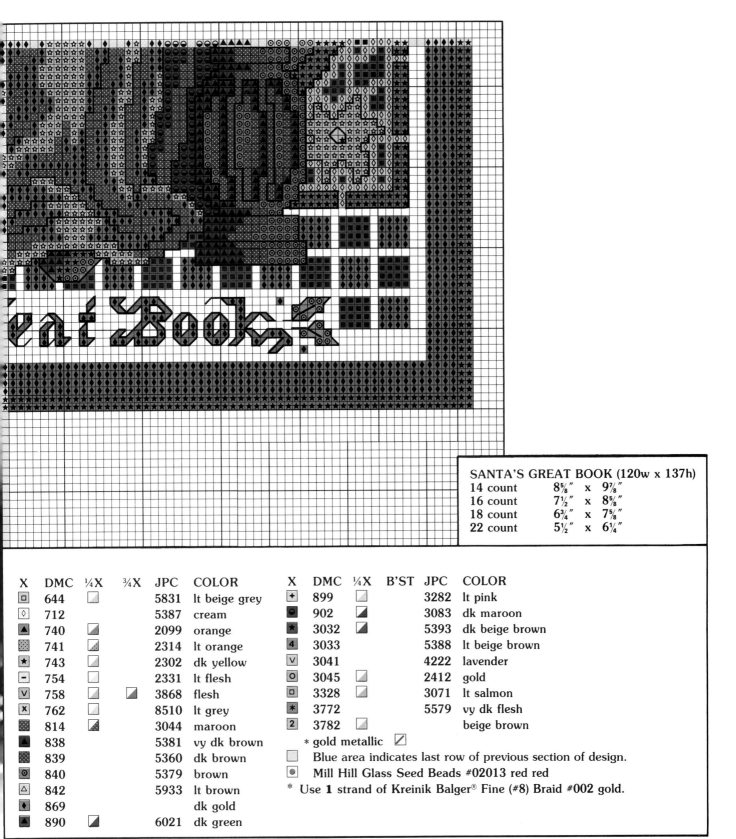

SANTA'S GREAT BOOK (120w x 137h)

14 count	$8\frac{5}{8}"$	x	$9\frac{7}{8}"$
16 count	$7\frac{1}{2}"$	x	$8\frac{5}{8}"$
18 count	$6\frac{3}{4}"$	x	$7\frac{5}{8}"$
22 count	$5\frac{1}{2}"$	x	$6\frac{1}{4}"$

X	DMC	¼X	¾X	JPC	COLOR
▫	644	◪		5831	lt beige grey
◇	712			5387	cream
▲	740	◪		2099	orange
▥	741	◪		2314	lt orange
★	743	◪		2302	dk yellow
-	754	◪		2331	lt flesh
V	758	◪	◪	3868	flesh
X	762	◪		8510	lt grey
▪	814	◪		3044	maroon
▲	838			5381	vy dk brown
▨	839			5360	dk brown
◉	840			5379	brown
△	842			5933	lt brown
◆	869				dk gold
▲	890	◪		6021	dk green

X	DMC	¼X	B'ST	JPC	COLOR
+	899	◪		3282	lt pink
◕	902	◪		3083	dk maroon
★	3032	◪		5393	dk beige brown
4	3033			5388	lt beige brown
V	3041			4222	lavender
◎	3045	◪		2412	gold
▫	3328	◪		3071	lt salmon
✳	3772			5579	vy dk flesh
2	3782	◪			beige brown

* gold metallic ◪

☐ Blue area indicates last row of previous section of design.

◉ Mill Hill Glass Seed Beads #02013 red red

* Use **1** strand of Kreinik Balger® Fine (#8) Braid #002 gold.

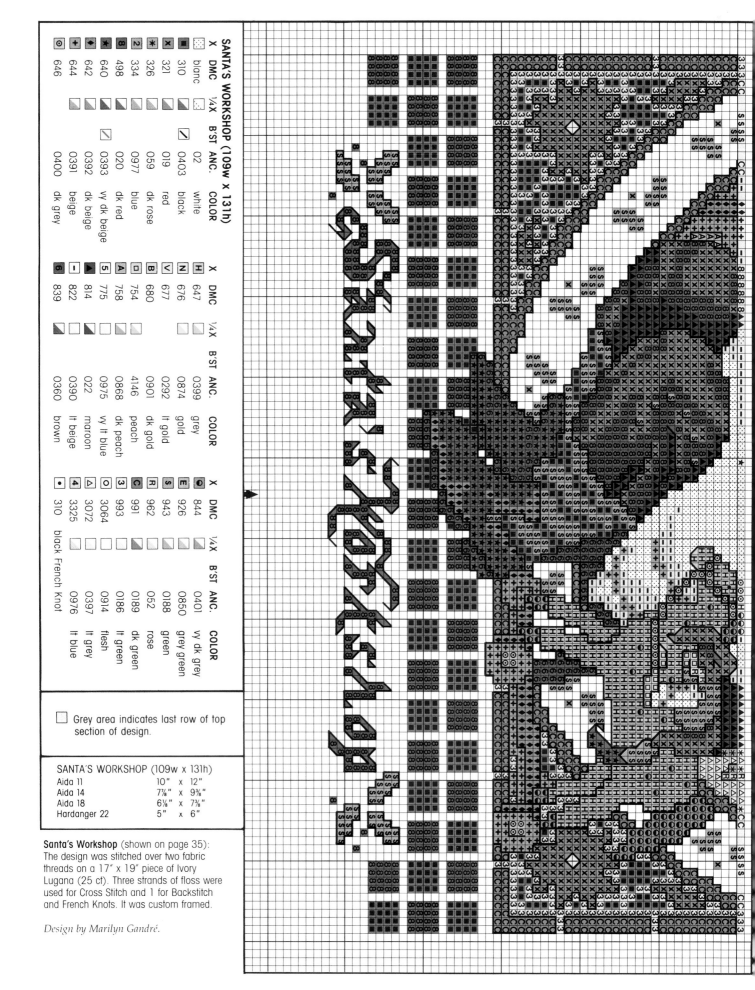

SANTA'S WORKSHOP (109w x 131h)

X	DMC	ANC.	COLOR
⊙	blanc	02	white
+	310	0403	black
◆	321	019	red
★	326	059	dk rose
8	334	977	blue
2	498	020	dk red
✕	640	0393	vy dk beige
▣	642	0392	dk beige
▨	644	0391	beige
⸬	646	0400	dk grey

X	DMC	ANC.	COLOR
H	647	0399	grey
N	676	0874	gold
V	677	0292	lt gold
B	680	0901	dk gold
□	754	4146	peach
A	758	0868	dk peach
5	775	0975	vy lt blue
▶	814	022	maroon
I	822	0390	lt beige
6	839	0360	brown

X	DMC	ANC.	COLOR
◑	844	0401	vy dk grey
E	926	0850	grey green
S	943	0188	green
R	962	052	rose
C	991	0189	dk green
3	993	0186	lt green
O	3064	0914	flesh
▷	3072	0397	lt grey
4	3325	0976	lt blue
•	310		black French Knot

Grey area indicates last row of top section of design.

SANTA'S WORKSHOP (109w x 131h)
Aida 11   10"   x 12"
Aida 14   7⅞"   x 9⅜"
Aida 18   6⅛"   x 7⅜"
Hardanger 22   5"   x 6"

Santa's Workshop (shown on page 35): The design was stitched over two fabric threads on a 17" x 19" piece of Ivory Lugana (25 ct). Three strands of floss were used for Cross Stitch and 1 for Backstitch and French Knots. It was custom framed.

Design by Marilyn Gandré.

TALLY HO HO HO (96w x 83h)

X	DMC	¼X	B'ST	JPC	COLOR
⠄	blanc	⠄		1001	white
✦	304			3401	dk red
▨	310		╱	8403	black
	310		╱ *	8403	black
◆	318			8511	dk grey
3	319			6246	green
✳	321	◢		3500	red
◉	350			3111	orange red
▦	413			8514	vy dk grey
★	415			8398	grey
▲	502	◸		6876	lt green
☆	504			6875	vy lt green
▬	666			3046	lt red
▒	725			2298	yellow

X	DMC	¼X	B'ST	JPC	COLOR
▬	726			2295	lt yellow
▨	754	◢		2331	peach
◉	760			3069	rose
△	761	◸		3068	lt rose
2	762		□	8510	lt grey
★	782		╱ *	5308	gold
◆	783			5307	lt gold
▨	815	◢		3000	vy dk red
◎	890	◢	╱	6021	dk green
8	928		□	7225	vy lt grey
✕	948		◸	2331	lt peach
☆	3712	◢			dk rose
S	3799			8999	charcoal grey
	* Use 2 strands of floss.				

TALLY HO HO HO (96w x 83h)

14 count	6⅞"	x	6"
16 count	6"	x	5¼"
18 count	5⅜"	x	4⅝"
22 count	4⅜"	x	3⅞"

Tally Ho Ho Ho (shown on page 37): The design was stitched over two fabric threads on a 12" x 11" piece of White Lugana (25 ct). Three strands of floss were used for Cross Stitch and 1 for Backstitch (unless otherwise indicated in color key). See Pillow Finishing, page 141.

Design by Vicky Howard. Needlework adaptation by Jane Chandler.

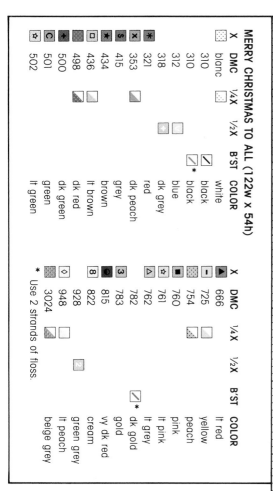

MERRY CHRISTMAS TO ALL (122w x 54h)

X	1/4X	1/2X	B'ST	DMC	COLOR
				blanc	white
				310	black
				310	black
				312	blue
				318	dk grey
				321	red
				353	dk peach
				415	grey
				434	brown
				436	lt brown
				498	dk red
				500	dk green
				501	green
				502	lt green

X	1/4X	1/2X	B'ST	DMC	COLOR
				666	lt red
				725	yellow
				754	peach
				760	pink
				761	lt pink
				762	lt grey
				782	dk gold
				783	gold
				815	vy dk red
				822	cream
				928	green grey
				948	lt peach
				3024	beige grey

* Use 2 strands of floss.

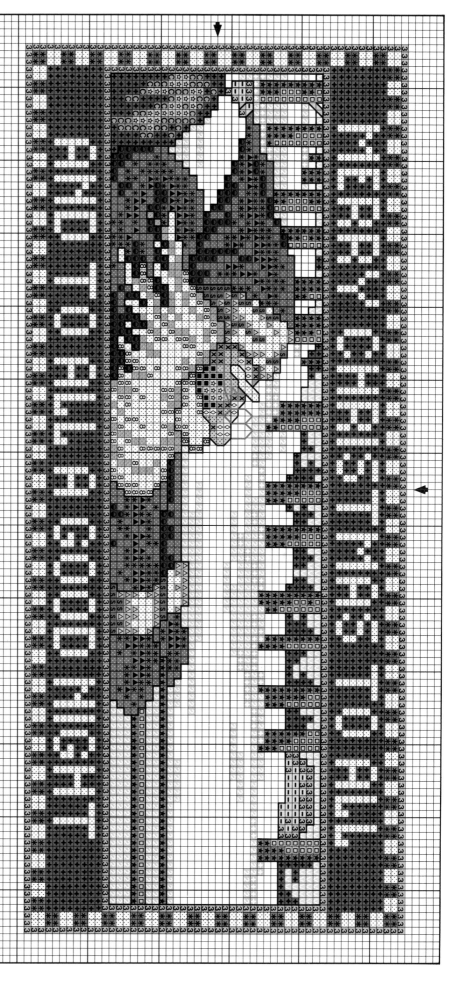

Merry Christmas To All (shown on page 36): The design was stitched over two fabric threads on a 14″ x 9″ piece of White Lugana (25 ct). Three strands of floss were used for Cross Stitch, 1 for Half Cross Stitch, and 1 for Backstitch (unless otherwise indicated in color key). It was made into a pillow.

For pillow front, center design and trim stitched piece to measure 11½″ x 6″.

(**Note:** Use ½″ seam allowance for all seams.)

For cording, cut one 2″ x 37″ bias strip of fabric. Center 37″ length of ¼″ dia. cord on wrong side of bias strip; matching long edges, fold strip over cord. Using zipper foot, baste along length of strip close to cord; trim seam allowance to ½″. Matching raw edges and beginning at bottom edge, pin cording to right side of pillow front, making a ³/₈″ clip in seam allowance of cording at each corner. Ends of cording should overlap approx. 2″; pin overlapping end out of the way. Starting 2″ from beginning end of cording and ending 4″ from overlapping end, sew cording to pillow front. On overlapping end of cording, remove 2½″ of basting; fold end of fabric back and trim cord so it meets beginning end of cord. Fold end of fabric under ½″; wrap fabric over beginning end of cording. Finish sewing cording to pillow front.

For ruffle, press short ends of a 2″ x 76″ strip of fabric ½″ to wrong side. Matching wrong sides and long edges, fold strip in half; press. Gather fabric strip to fit pillow front. Matching raw edges and beginning at bottom edge, pin ruffle to right side of pillow front overlapping short ends ¼″; sew ruffle to pillow front.

For pillow back, cut an 11½″ X 6″ piece of coordinating fabric. Matching right sides and leaving an opening for turning, sew pillow front and pillow back together. Trim corners diagonally. Turn pillow right side out, carefully pushing corners outward. Stuff pillow with polyester fiberfill and sew final closure by hand.

Design by Vicky Howard.
Needlework adaptation by Jane Chandler.

SANTA (139w x 110h)

Aida 11	12¾"	x	10"
Aida 14	10"	x	7⅞"
Aida 18	7¾"	x	6⅛"
Hardanger 22	6⅜"	x	5"

☐ Blue area indicates first row of next section of design.

110

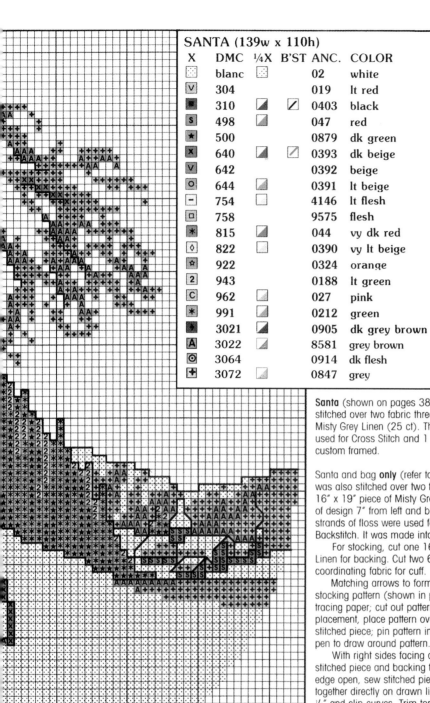

X	DMC	¼X	B'ST	ANC.	COLOR
(dotted)	blanc	(dotted)		02	white
V	304			019	lt red
■	310	◪	◿	0403	black
S	498	◪		047	red
★	500			0879	dk green
X	640	◪	◿	0393	dk beige
V	642			0392	beige
○	644	◪		0391	lt beige
−	754		◻	4146	lt flesh
◻	758			9575	flesh
＊	815	◪		044	vy dk red
◊	822		◻	0390	vy lt beige
☆	922			0324	orange
2	943			0188	lt green
C	962	◪		027	pink
＊	991	◪		0212	green
◪	3021	◪		0905	dk grey brown
A	3022	◪		8581	grey brown
◉	3064			0914	dk flesh
✛	3072	◪		0847	grey

SANTA (139w x 110h)

Santa (shown on pages 38-39): The design was stitched over two fabric threads on a 19″ x 17″ piece of Misty Grey Linen (25 ct). Three strands of floss were used for Cross Stitch and 1 for Backstitch. It was custom framed.

Santa and bag **only** (refer to photo on pages 38-39) was also stitched over two fabric threads on a 16″ x 19″ piece of Misty Grey Linen (25 ct) with center of design 7″ from left and bottom edges of fabric. Three strands of floss were used for Cross Stitch and 1 for Backstitch. It was made into a stocking.

For stocking, cut one 16″ x 19″ piece of Misty Grey Linen for backing. Cut two 6¼″ x 4¾″ pieces of coordinating fabric for cuff.

Matching arrows to form one pattern, trace entire stocking pattern (shown in pink on page 142) onto tracing paper; cut out pattern. Referring to photo for placement, place pattern over design on wrong side of stitched piece; pin pattern in place. Use fabric marking pen to draw around pattern. Do **not** cut out.

With right sides facing and matching raw edges, pin stitched piece and backing fabric together. Leaving top edge open, sew stitched piece and backing fabric together directly on drawn line. Trim seam allowance to ½″ and clip curves. Trim top edge along drawn line. Do not turn stocking right side out.

Matching right sides and using a ¼″ seam allowance, sew cuff pieces together along short edges. Press one long edge of cuff ¼″ to wrong side; press ¼″ to wrong side again and hem.

With right side of cuff and wrong side of stocking facing, match raw edges and use a ¼″ seam allowance to sew cuff to stocking. Turn stocking right side out. Fold cuff 3″ over stocking; press.

For hanger, fold a 2″ length of ¼″w grosgrain ribbon in half. Whipstitch to inside of stocking at left seam.

Design by Marilyn Gandré.

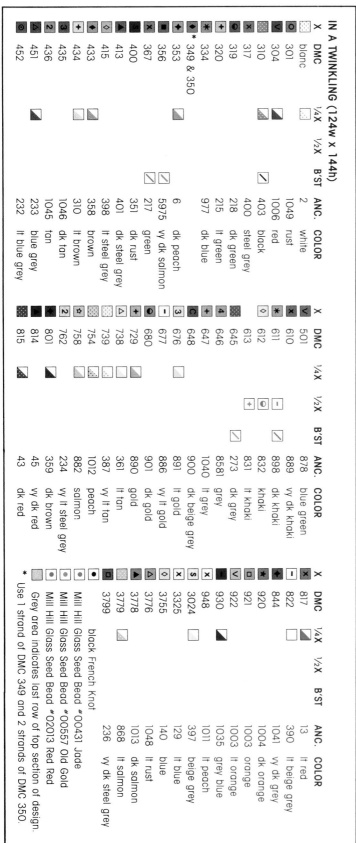

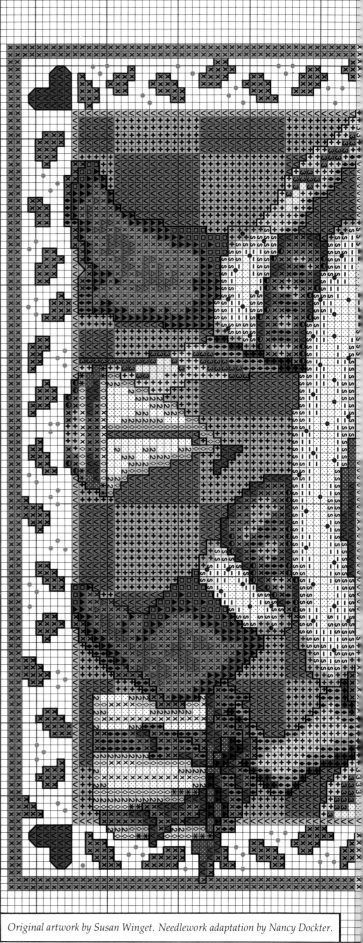

IN A TWINKLING (124w x 144h)

X	¼X	½X	B'ST	DMC	ANC.	COLOR
				blanc	2	white
				301	1049	rust
				304	1006	red
				310	403	black
				317	400	steel grey
				319	218	dk green
				320	215	lt green
				334	977	dk blue
				*349 & 350		
				353	6	dk peach
				356	5975	vy dk salmon
				367	217	green
				400	351	dk rust
				413	401	dk steel grey
				415	398	lt steel grey
				433	358	brown
				434	310	lt brown
				435	1046	dk tan
				436	1045	tan
				451	233	blue grey
				452	232	lt blue grey

X	¼X	½X	B'ST	DMC	ANC.	COLOR
				501	878	blue green
				610	889	vy dk khaki
				611	898	dk khaki
				612	832	khaki
				613	831	lt khaki
				645	273	dk grey
				646	8581	grey
				647	1040	lt grey
				648	900	lt beige grey
				676	891	lt gold
				677	886	vy lt gold
				680	901	dk gold
				729	890	gold
				738	361	lt tan
				739	387	vy lt tan
				754	1012	peach
				758	882	salmon
				762	234	vy lt steel grey
				801	359	dk brown
				814	45	vy dk red
				815	43	dk red

X	¼X	½X	B'ST	DMC	ANC.	COLOR
				817	13	lt red
				822	390	lt beige grey
				844	1041	vy dk grey
				920	1004	dk orange
				921	1003	orange
				922	1003	lt orange
				930	1035	grey blue
				948	1011	lt peach
				3024	397	beige grey
				3325	129	lt blue
				3755	140	blue
				3776	1048	lt rust
				3778	1013	dk salmon
				3779	868	vy lt salmon
				3799	236	vy dk steel grey
						black French Knot
						Mill Hill Glass Seed Bead #00431 Jade
						Mill Hill Glass Seed Bead #00557 Old Gold
						Mill Hill Glass Seed Bead #02013 Red Red

* Grey area indicates last row of top section of design. Use 1 strand of DMC 349 and 2 strands of DMC 350.

In A Twinkling (shown on pages 40-41): The design was stitched over two fabric threads on an 18" x 20" piece of Mushroom Lugana (25 ct). Three strands of floss were used for Cross Stitch (unless otherwise indicated in color key) and 1 for Backstitch and French Knots. It was custom framed.

Original artwork by Susan Winget. Needlework adaptation by Nancy Dockter.

SANTA REUNION (150w x 95h)

X	DMC	¼X	½X	B'ST	ANC.	COLOR
⠫	blanc	⠂		◹	2	white
★	301	◸			1049	dk rust
▩	304	◪			1006	red
▩	310	◪		◹	403	black
▲	311	◺			148	dk blue
⊙	312	◺		◹	979	blue
◨	319	◺			218	dk green
○	320	▢			215	lt green
▢	321	◻			9046	lt red
◆	322				978	lt blue
◆	326				59	rose
✦	333	◺			119	dk violet
+	341	▢			117	lt violet
△	367	◺			217	green
☆	402	▢			1047	lt rust
	413			◹	401	dk grey
▲	433				358	brown
⊟	434	◺			310	lt brown
✳	437	▢			362	tan
▩	451	◪			233	shell grey
◇	453	◺			231	lt shell grey
△	498				1005	dk red
✳	642				392	dk beige grey
⊕	644				830	beige grey
▢	645	◺			273	green grey
	647		◻		1040	lt green grey
−	666	▢			46	vy lt red
×	676	▢			891	lt gold
○	725	▢		◹	305	yellow
⠫	754	⠂			1012	flesh
✳	760	◺			1022	pink
◆	783	◺			307	gold
▩	814	◪		◹	45	dk maroon
⊕	815	◺			43	maroon
▩	816				1005	lt maroon
▲	822	◺			390	lt beige grey
★	844	◺			1041	dk green grey
■	902				897	vy dk maroon
✦	3345				268	dk yellow green
−	3346				267	yellow green
×	3347	▢			266	lt yellow green
△	3348	▢			264	vy lt yellow green
☆	3746	◺			1030	violet
⊕	3776	◺			1048	rust
●	310				403	black Fr. Knot
●	312				979	blue Fr. Knot
●	666				46	vy lt red Fr. Knot
●	725				305	yellow Fr. Knot
●	814				45	dk maroon Fr. Knot
⊘	676				891	lt gold Lazy Daisy
▢						Blue area indicates first row of right section of design.

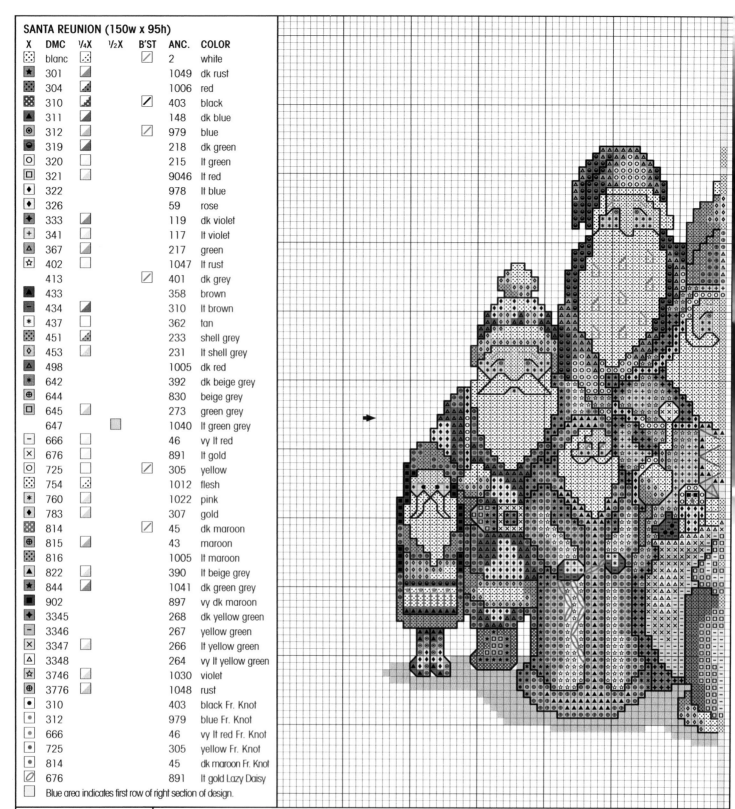

SANTA REUNION (150w x 95h)

14 count	10¾"	x	6⅞"
16 count	9⅜"	x	6"
18 count	8⅜"	x	5⅜"
22 count	6⅞"	x	4⅜"

Santa Reunion (shown on pages 42-43): The design was stitched on a 19" x 15" piece of Ivory Aida (14 ct). Three strands of floss were used for Cross Stitch, 1 for Half Cross Stitch and French Knots, 2 for Backstitch eyebrows and 1 for all other Backstitch. It was custom framed.

Design by Heartprint, Inc.

SANTA BRINGS GOOD CHEER (96w x 132h)

X	DMC	¼X	½X	B'ST	ANC.	COLOR
	blanc				2	white
	310			⊠*	403	black
	414				235	dk grey
	415				398	grey
	434				310	dk tan
	435				1046	tan
	437				362	lt tan
	498				1005	dk red
	500				683	vy dk blue green
	501				878	dk blue green
	502				877	blue green
	503				876	lt blue green
	504				1042	vy lt blue green
	518				1039	blue
	597				168	lt blue
	598				167	vy lt blue
	610				889	dk beige
	611				898	dk beige
	613				831	beige
	642				392	khaki
	644				830	lt beige
	666				46	lt red
	725				305	yellow
	727				293	lt yellow
	754				1012	lt flesh
	758				882	flesh

X	DMC	¼X	½X	B'ST	ANC.	COLOR
	760				1022	pink
	762				234	lt grey
	782				308	dk gold
	783				307	gold
	801			⊠†	359	brown
	814				45	vy dk red
	817				13	red
	822				390	ecru
	892				33	vy dk pink
	893				28	dk pink
	894				27	lt pink
	938			⊠	381	dk brown
	948				1011	vy lt flesh
	3021				905	dk grey brown
	3362				263	dk green
	3363				262	green
	3364				260	lt green
	3750			⊠	1036	vy dk blue
	3761				928	sky blue
	3765				170	dk blue
	3778				1013	dk flesh
	3781			⊠	1050	dk grey brown
	3787				310	dk khaki

• 310 black French Knot

* For drum laces, work in long stitches.

† For framed piece, use 2 strands.

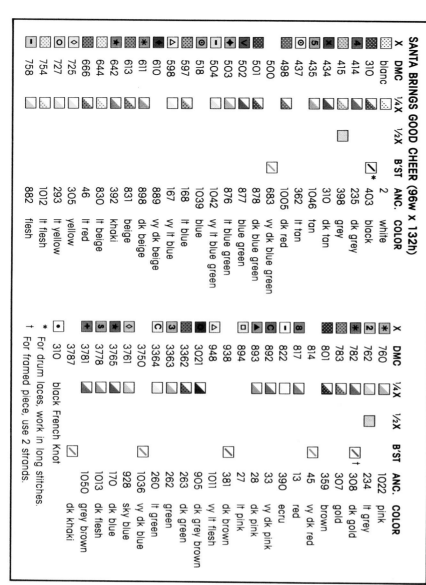
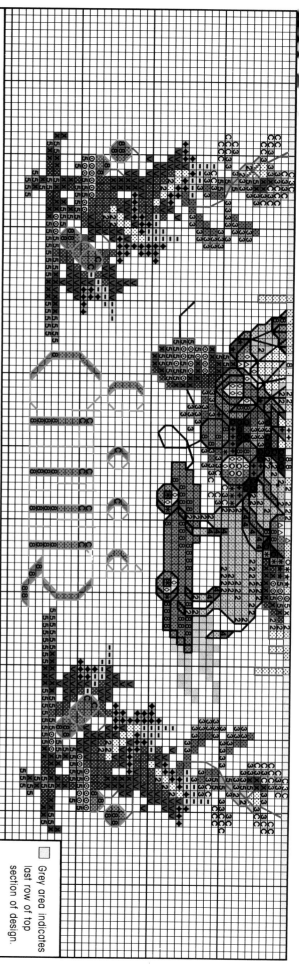

Grey area indicates last row of top section of design.

Santa Brings Good Cheer (shown on pages 44-45): The design was stitched over two fabric threads on a 13" x 16" piece of Natural Irish Linen (28 ct). Three strands of floss were used for Cross Stitch and 1 for Half Cross Stitch, Backstitch and French Knots (unless otherwise indicated in color key). It was custom framed.

Design by Donna Vermillion Giampa.

SANTA BRINGS GOOD CHEER (96w x 132h)

14 count	6⅞"	x 9½"
16 count	6"	x 8¼"
18 count	5⅜"	x 7⅜"
22 count	4⅜"	x 6"

X	DMC	¼X	B'ST	ANC.	COLOR
▨	blanc	▨	╱	2	white
■	310		╱	403	black
▨	318	▨		399	grey
⊙	319			218	green
▽	320			215	lt green
✕	414	◪		235	dk grey
◆	415	◪		398	lt grey
⊙	422	☐		373	tan
✛	642			392	dk beige grey
⊟	644	◪		830	beige grey
◇	676			891	gold
○	677		╱	886	lt gold
☆	729			890	dk gold
✛	754			1012	peach
⊕	760	◪		1022	coral
▲	761			1021	lt coral
☆	762	◪		234	vy lt grey

X	DMC	¼X	B'ST	ANC.	COLOR
▢	775	◪		128	vy lt blue
⊕	822	◪		390	lt beige grey
★	869	◪	╱	944	brown
⊟	930	◪	╱	1035	dk blue
✕	931			1034	blue
▨	932	▨		1033	lt blue
−	948	☐		1011	lt peach
◆	3045	◪		888	yellow beige
▢	3047	◪		852	lt yellow beige
▨	3064			883	dk peach
▲	3350	◪	╱	59	pink
◇	3354			74	lt pink
✳	3685			1028	dk pink
●	310			403	black Fr. Knot
▨					Pink area indicates first row of next section of design.

PRAIRIE SANTA (136w x 120h)

Aida 11	12³/₈"	x	11"
Aida 14	9³/₄"	x	8⁵/₈"
Aida 18	7⁵/₈"	x	6³/₄"
Hardanger 22	6¹/₄"	x	5¹/₂"

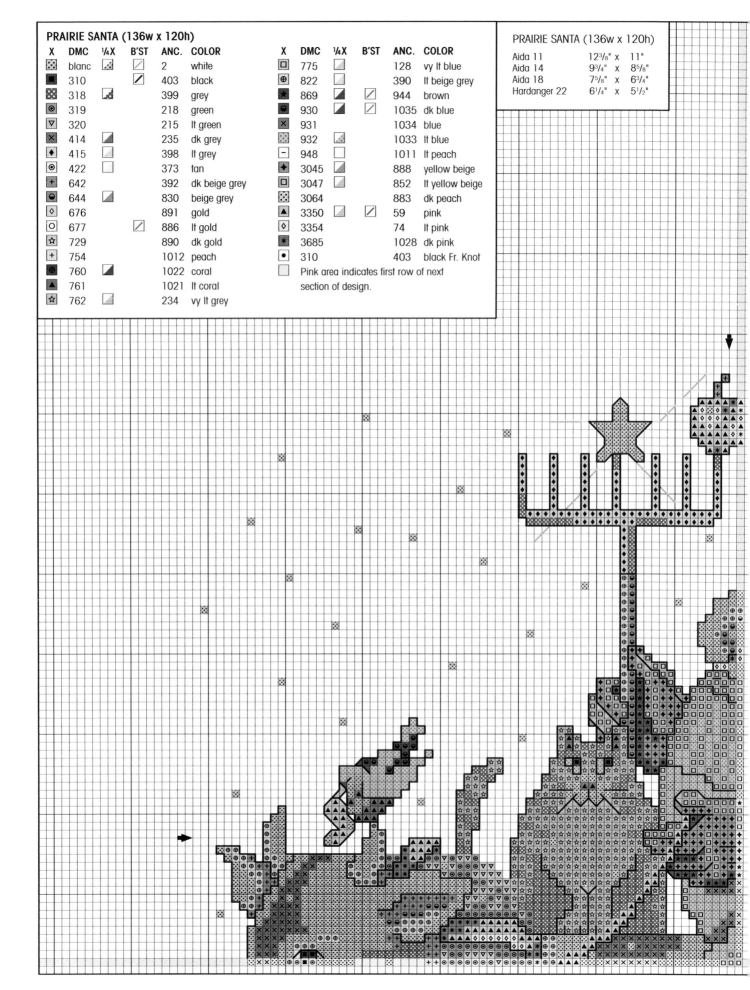

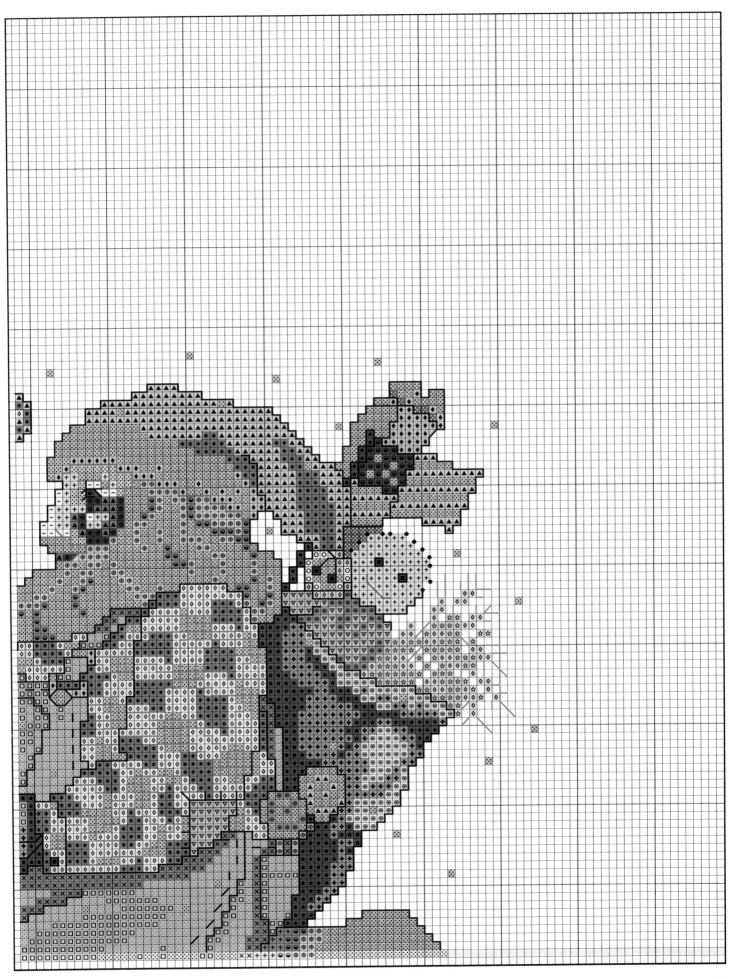

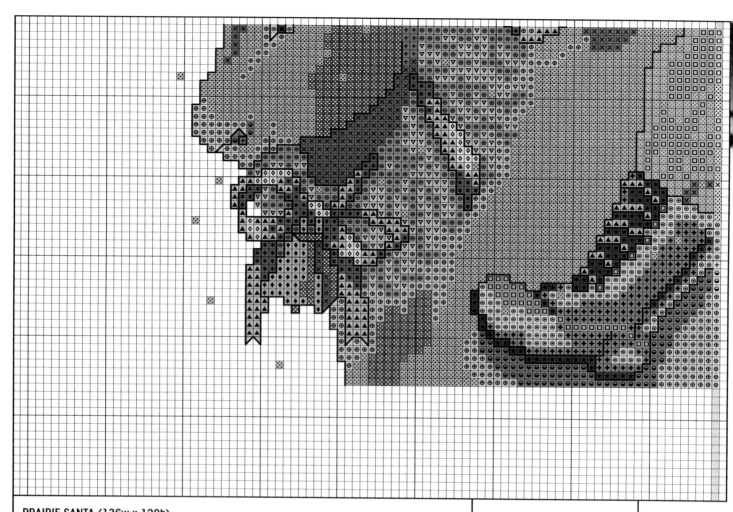

PRAIRIE SANTA (136w x 120h)

X	DMC	1/4X	B'ST	ANC.	COLOR
▨	blanc	◩	◪	2	white
■	310		◪	403	black
▨	318	◩		399	grey
⊙	319			218	green
▽	320			215	lt green
✕	414	◪		235	dk grey
◆	415	◪		398	lt grey
⊙	422	◪		373	tan
✛	642			392	dk beige grey
◕	644	◪		830	beige grey
◇	676			891	gold
○	677		◪	886	lt gold
☆	729			890	dk gold
✛	754			1012	peach
⊕	760	◪		1022	coral
▲	761			1021	lt coral
☆	762	◪		234	vy lt grey

X	DMC	1/4X	B'ST	ANC.	COLOR
▢	775	◪		128	vy lt blue
⊕	822	◪		390	lt beige grey
★	869	◪	◪	944	brown
◕	930	◪	◪	1035	dk blue
✕	931			1034	blue
▨	932	◩		1033	lt blue
–	948	▢		1011	lt peach
✦	3045	◪		888	yellow beige
▢	3047	◪		852	lt yellow beige
▨	3064			883	dk peach
▲	3350	◪	◪	59	pink
◇	3354			74	lt pink
✳	3685			1028	dk pink
•	310			403	black Fr. Knot
▨					Pink area indicates first row of next section of design.

PRAIRIE SANTA (136w x 120h)

Aida 11	12³/₈" x	11"
Aida 14	9³/₄" x	8⁵/₈"
Aida 18	7⁵/₈" x	6³/₄"
Hardanger 22	6¹/₄" x	5¹/₂"

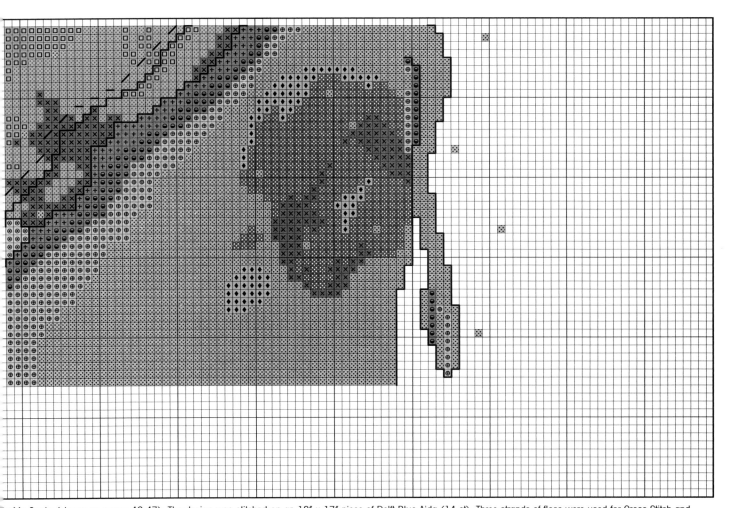

Prairie Santa (shown on pages 46-47): The design was stitched on an 18″ x 17″ piece of Delft Blue Aida (14 ct). Three strands of floss were used for Cross Stitch and for Backstitch and French Knots. It was custom framed.

Design by Sandi Gore Evans.

BE JOLLY (105w x 105h)
TREE (23w x 21h)
SANTA (22w x 22h)

X	DMC	¼X	B'ST	ANC.	COLOR
	blanc	¼X		02	white
▲	224			0893	mauve
✚	225	¼X		0892	lt mauve
■	310	¼X	B'ST	0403	black
▲	318	¼X		0399	grey
	319		B'ST	0217	dk green
★	367	¼X		0216	green
✚	368	¼X		0214	lt green
	414		B'ST	0400	dk grey
◎	415	¼X		0398	lt grey
◉	420	¼X		0375	dk hazel brown
Ⓐ	422			0373	lt hazel brown
▨	640	¼X		0393	beige grey
▫	676	¼X		0891	gold
▫	677	¼X		0300	lt gold
	729			0890	dk gold
◎	754	¼X		4146	flesh
◉	760	¼X		09	salmon
▨	761	¼X		08	lt salmon
◆	801	¼X	B'ST	0358	brown
✕	816	¼X		019	red
◖	842	¼X		0376	beige
✿	869	¼X		0906	vy dk hazel brown
◉	902	¼X	B'ST	022	maroon
✕	927	¼X		0849	dk blue grey
◎	928	¼X		0847	blue grey

X	DMC	¼X	ANC.	COLOR
▲	931	¼X	0921	blue
✚	932	¼X	0920	lt blue
-	948		0778	lt flesh
◣	991	¼X	0188	dk aqua
▽	992		0187	aqua
◯	993	¼X	0186	lt aqua
★	3021		0905	dk beige grey
✳	3032		0832	lt beige grey
▨	3033	¼X	0830	vy lt beige grey
▨	3045		0888	hazel brown
▨	3046	¼X	0887	yellow beige
◬	3052		0859	olive
◎	3350	¼X	059	dk pink
◎	3354	¼X	050	pink
◆	3685	¼X	069	dk rose
▫	3687	¼X	068	rose
▨	3688		066	lt rose
●	blanc		02	white Fr. Knot
●	310		0403	black Fr. Knot
●	902		022	maroon Fr. Knot
●	930		0922	dk blue Fr. Knot
●	991		0188	dk aqua Fr. Knot
⊘	367		0216	green Lazy Daisy
⊘	676		0891	gold Lazy Daisy
⊘	930		0922	dk blue Lazy Daisy

☐ Blue area indicates first row of next section of design.

BE JOLLY (105w x 105h)	
Aida 11	9⅝" x 9⅝"
Aida 14	7½" x 7½"
Aida 18	5⅞" x 5⅞"
Hardanger 22	4⅞" x 4⅞"

TREE (23w x 21h)	
Aida 11	2⅛" x 2"
Aida 14	1¾" x 1½"
Aida 18	1⅜" x 1¼"
Hardanger 22	1⅛" x 1"

SANTA (22w x 22h)	
Aida 11	2" x 2"
Aida 14	1⅝" x 1⅝"
Aida 18	1¼" x 1¼"
Hardanger 22	1" x 1"

Be Jolly (shown on pages 48-49): The design was stitched over two fabric threads on a 17″ square of Ivory Lugana (25 ct). Three strands of floss were used for Cross Stitch and 1 for Backstitch, French Knots, and Lazy Daisy Stitches. It was custom framed.

Each design (shown on pages 48-49) was stitched over two fabric threads on a 6″ square of Ivory Lugana (25 ct). Three strands of floss were used for Cross Stitch and 1 for Backstitch and French Knots. See Mini Pillow Finishing, page 141.

Design by Diane Brakefield.

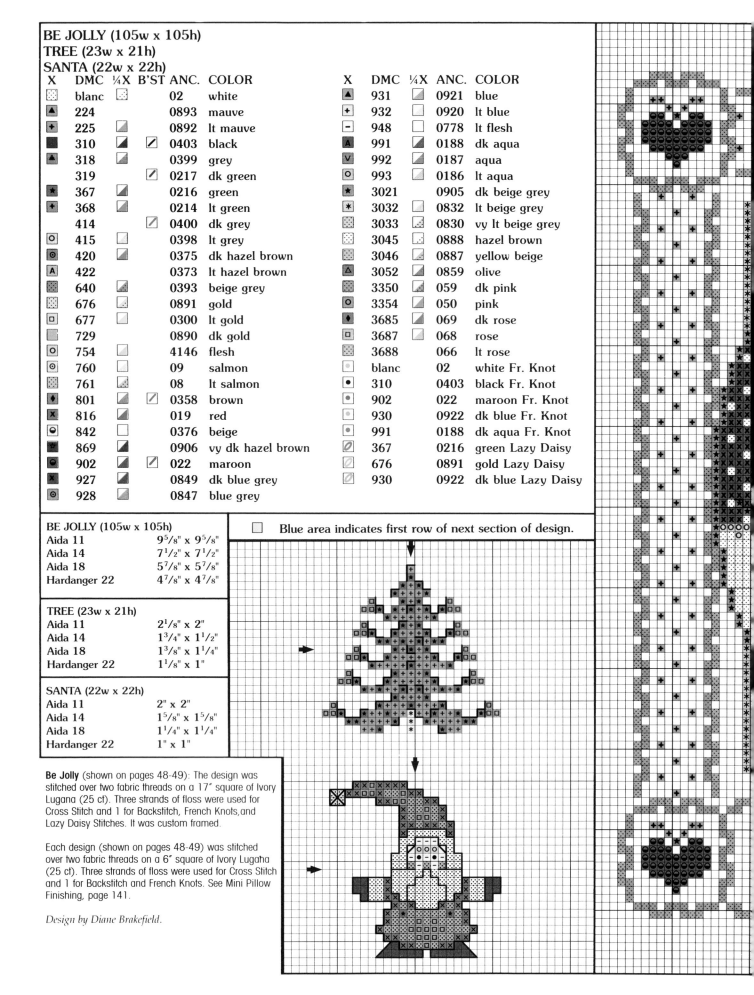

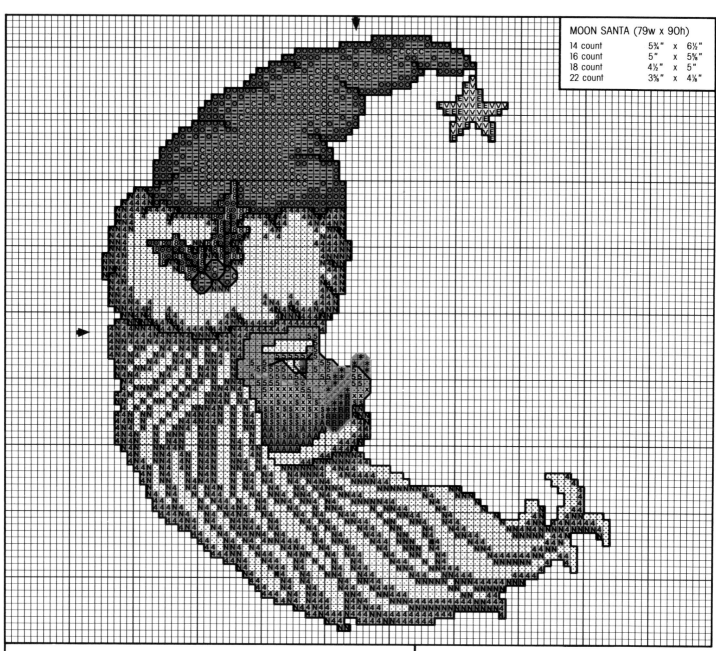

MOON SANTA (79w x 90h)

	14 count	5¾"	x	6½"
	16 count	5"	x	5⅝"
	18 count	4½"	x	5"
	22 count	3⅝"	x	4⅛"

MOON SANTA (79w x 90h)

X	DMC	¼X	B'ST	JPC	COLOR		X	DMC	¼X	B'ST	JPC	COLOR
	blanc		✓	1001	white		x	761			3068	vy lt salmon
O	304	◣		3401	dk red		4	762			8510	vy lt grey
+	310		✓	8403	black		E	783		✓	5307	gold
-	321	◣		3500	red		R	927	◣		6006	blue grey
	322			7978	blue		*	928	◣		7225	lt blue grey
N	415	◣		8398	lt grey		5	948	◣		2331	lt peach
C	666			3046	lt red		O	986	◣		6021	green
V	725			2298	yellow		8	988	◣		6258	lt green
	754	◣		3146	peach		A	3712				salmon
S	760	◣		3069	lt salmon		•	blanc				white French Knot

Moon Santa (shown on page 50): The design was stitched on an 11" square of Antique White Aida (14 ct) with design placed 1¼" from the left side and 1¼" from the bottom edge of fabric piece. Three strands of floss were used for Cross Stitch, 4 for gold Backstitch and 1 for Backstitch and French Knot. It was made into a pillow.

For pillow, cut one piece of fabric the same size as stitched piece for backing. For ruffle, press short ends of a 5" x 80" strip of fabric ½" to wrong side. Matching wrong sides and long edges, fold strip in half; press. Gather fabric strip to fit stitched piece. Matching raw edges and beginning at bottom edge, pin ruffle to right side of stitched piece overlapping short ends ¼". Using ½" seam allowance, sew ruffle to stitched piece. Matching right sides and leaving an opening for turning, use a ½" seam allowance to sew stitched piece and backing fabric together. Trim corners diagonally. Turn pillow right side out, carefully pushing corners outward. Stuff pillow with polyester fiberfill and sew final closure by hand.

Design by Vicky Howard.

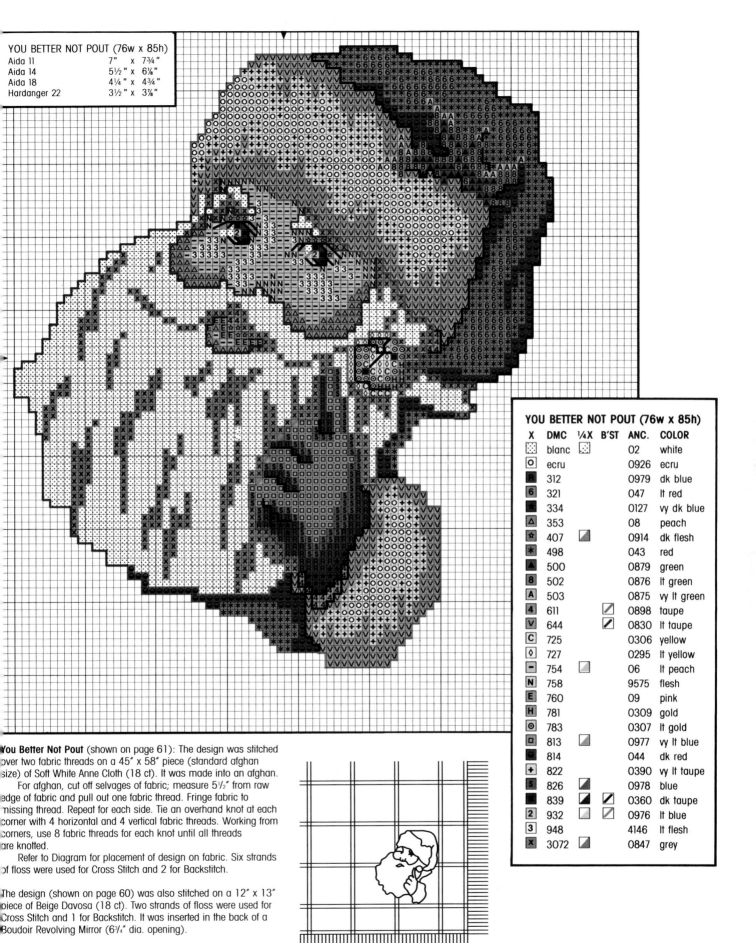

YOU BETTER NOT POUT (76w x 85h)

Aida 11	7" x 7¾"
Aida 14	5½" x 6⅛"
Aida 18	4¼" x 4¾"
Hardanger 22	3½" x 3⅞"

YOU BETTER NOT POUT (76w x 85h)

X	DMC	¼X	B'ST	ANC.	COLOR
▨	blanc	▨		02	white
O	ecru			0926	ecru
R	312			0979	dk blue
6	321			047	lt red
✳	334			0127	vy dk blue
△	353			08	peach
☆	407	◪		0914	dk flesh
✳	498			043	red
▲	500			0879	green
8	502			0876	lt green
A	503			0875	vy lt green
4	611		◪	0898	taupe
V	644		◪	0830	lt taupe
C	725			0306	yellow
◊	727			0295	lt yellow
−	754	◪		06	lt peach
N	758			9575	flesh
E	760			09	pink
H	781			0309	gold
⊙	783			0307	lt gold
□	813	◪		0977	vy lt blue
◨	814			044	dk red
+	822			0390	vy lt taupe
S	826	◪		0978	blue
■	839	◪	◪	0360	dk taupe
2	932	◪	◪	0976	lt blue
3	948			4146	lt flesh
X	3072	◪		0847	grey

You Better Not Pout (shown on page 61): The design was stitched over two fabric threads on a 45" x 58" piece (standard afghan size) of Soft White Anne Cloth (18 ct). It was made into an afghan.

For afghan, cut off selvages of fabric; measure 5½" from raw edge of fabric and pull out one fabric thread. Fringe fabric to missing thread. Repeat for each side. Tie an overhand knot at each corner with 4 horizontal and 4 vertical fabric threads. Working from corners, use 8 fabric threads for each knot until all threads are knotted.

Refer to Diagram for placement of design on fabric. Six strands of floss were used for Cross Stitch and 2 for Backstitch.

The design (shown on page 60) was also stitched on a 12" x 13" piece of Beige Davosa (18 ct). Two strands of floss were used for Cross Stitch and 1 for Backstitch. It was inserted in the back of a Boudoir Revolving Mirror (6¾" dia. opening).

Design by Carol Emmer.

125

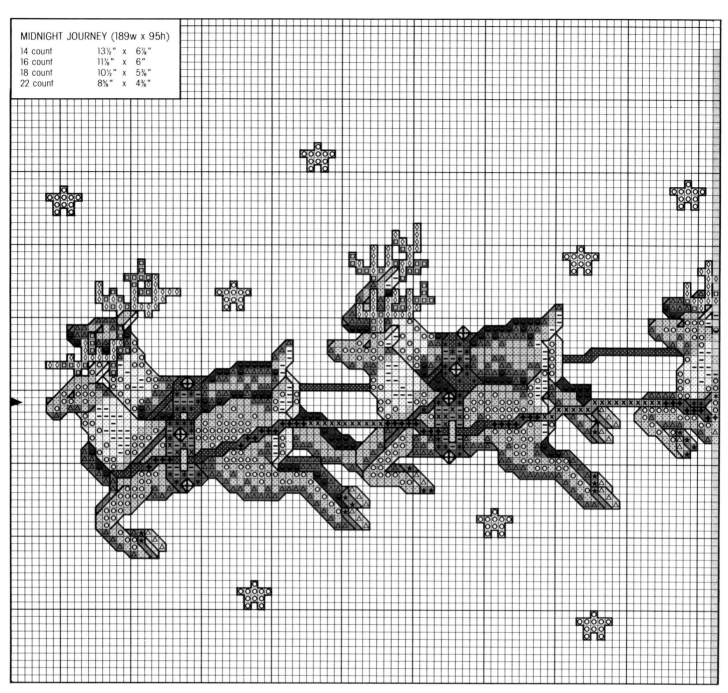

MIDNIGHT JOURNEY (189w x 95h)

14 count	13½"	x	6⅞"
16 count	11⅞"	x	6"
18 count	10½"	x	5⅜"
22 count	8⅝"	x	4⅜"

Midnight Journey (shown on page 51): The design was stitched over two fabric threads on a 45″ x 58″ piece (standard afghan size) of Royal Blue Anne Cloth (18 ct). It was made into an afghan.

For afghan, cut off selvages of fabric; measure 5½″ from raw edge of fabric and pull out one fabric thread. Fringe fabric up to missing thread. Repeat for each side. Tie an overhand knot at each corner with 4 horizontal and 4 vertical fabric threads. Working from corners, use 8 fabric threads for each knot until all threads are knotted.

Refer to Diagram for placement of design on fabric. Six strands of floss were used for Cross Stitch and 2 for Backstitch and French Knots (unless otherwise indicated in color key).

Original artwork by Peggy Jo Ackley for Family Line Greetings, Inc. Needlework adaptation by Jane Chandler.

Diagram

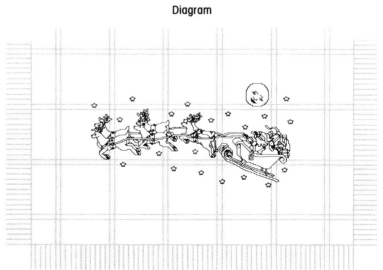

126

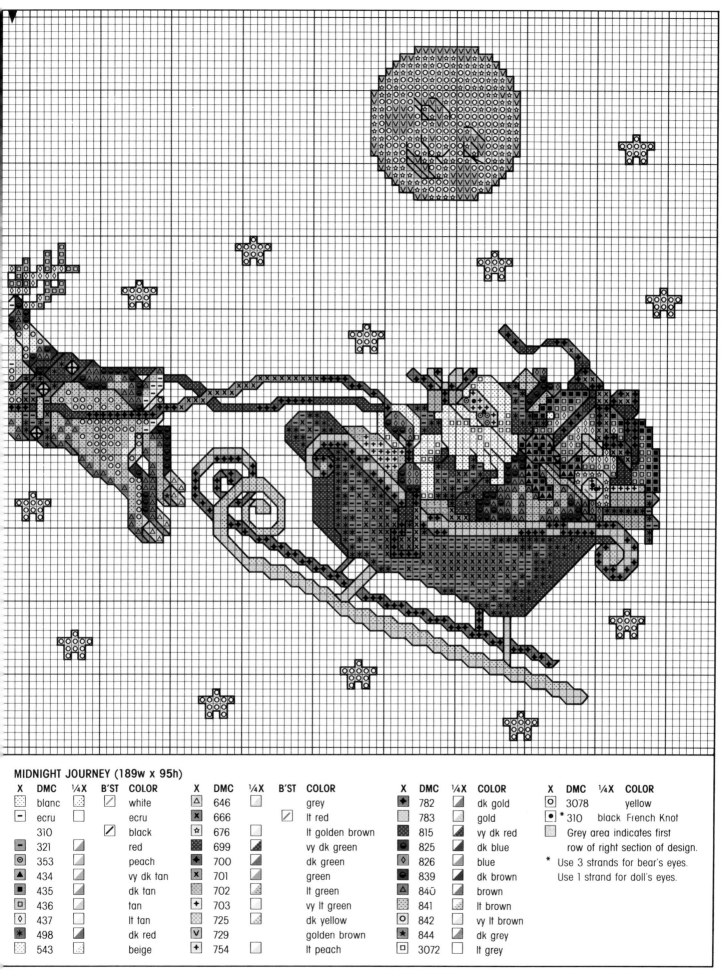

MIDNIGHT JOURNEY (189w x 95h)

X	DMC	¼X	B'ST	COLOR	X	DMC	¼X	B'ST	COLOR	X	DMC	¼X	COLOR	X	DMC	¼X	COLOR
	blanc			white	△	646			grey	◆	782		dk gold	○	3078		yellow
−	ecru			ecru	✕	666			lt red		783		gold	●	* 310		black French Knot
	310			black	☆	676			lt golden brown		815		vy dk red				Grey area indicates first
−	321			red		699			vy dk green	●	825		dk blue				row of right section of design.
⊙	353			peach	◆	700			dk green	◇	826		blue	*			Use 3 strands for bear's eyes.
▲	434			vy dk tan	✕	701			green	●	839		dk brown				Use 1 strand for doll's eyes.
■	435			dk tan		702			lt green	△	840		brown				
□	436			tan	✛	703			vy lt green		841		lt brown				
◇	437			lt tan		725			dk yellow	○	842		vy lt brown				
✳	498			dk red	∨	729			golden brown	★	844		dk grey				
	543			beige	✛	754			lt peach	□	3072		lt grey				

127

Santa on the Roof (shown on pages 52-53): The design was stitched over two fabric threads on a 21" x 15" piece of Navy Lugana (25 ct). Three strands of floss were used for Cross Stitch and 1 for Backstitch and French Knots. It was custom framed.

Santa **only** (shown on page 53) was also stitched over two fabric threads on a 10" x 13" piece of Ivory Aida (18 ct). Five strands of floss were used for Cross Stitch and 2 for Backstitch and French Knots. See Stuffed Figure Finishing, page 141.

Design by Susan Winget.

SANTA ON THE ROOF (160w x 87h)

X	DMC	¼X	¾X	B'ST	JPC	COLOR	X	DMC	¼X	¾X	B'ST	JPC	COLOR
	blanc				1001	white	N	435				5371	brown
O	ecru				1002	ecru	◊	436				5943	lt brown
■	310				8403	black	C	498				3410	red
▲	319				6246	dk green	★	676				2305	lt yellow
X	320				6017	lt green	8	677					vy lt yellow
*	347				3013	lt red		680					dk yellow
2	353				3006	peach	H	729				5363	yellow
⊙	367				6018	green	S	738				5375	tan
3	368				6016	vy lt green	4	739				5369	lt tan
■	434				5000	dk brown	-	754				2331	lt peach

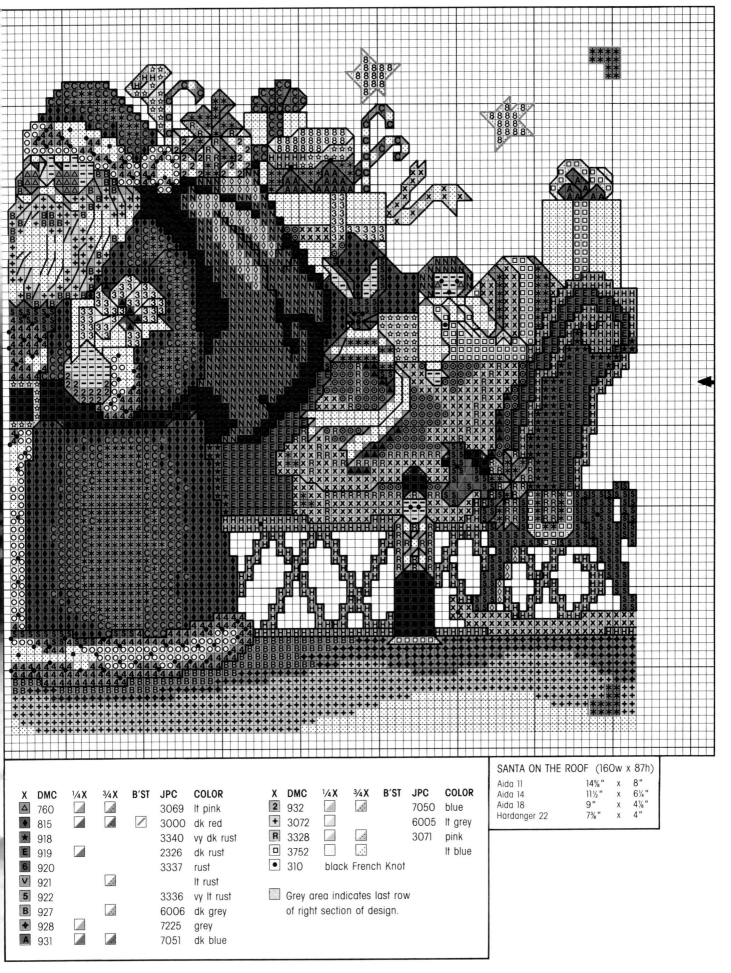

X	DMC	¼X	¾X	B'ST	JPC	COLOR
△	760	◪	◪		3069	lt pink
◆	815	◪	◪	◪	3000	dk red
★	918				3340	vy dk rust
E	919	◪			2326	dk rust
6	920				3337	rust
V	921		◪			lt rust
5	922				3336	vy lt rust
B	927		◪		6006	dk grey
◆	928	◪			7225	grey
A	931	◪	◪		7051	dk blue

X	DMC	¼X	¾X	B'ST	JPC	COLOR
2	932	◪	◪		7050	blue
+	3072	◪			6005	lt grey
R	3328	◪	◪		3071	pink
□	3752	◪	◪			lt blue
●	310		black French Knot			

◪ Grey area indicates last row
  of right section of design.

SANTA ON THE ROOF (160w x 87h)

Aida 11	14⅝"	x	8"
Aida 14	11½"	x	6¼"
Aida 18	9"	x	4⅞"
Hardanger 22	7⅜"	x	4"

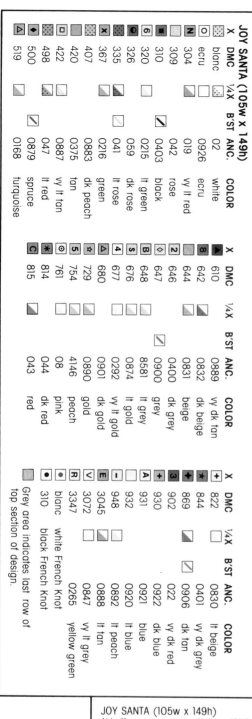

JOY SANTA (105w x 149h)

X	DMC	¼X	B'ST	ANC.	COLOR
	blanc	◩		02	white
O	ecru	◩		0926	ecru
N	304	◩		019	vy lt red
	309			042	rose
■	310		◩	0403	black
6	320	◩		0215	lt green
◒	326			059	dk rose
	335	◩	◩	041	lt rose
×	367	◩		0216	green
	407			0883	dk peach
	420			0375	tan
□	422	◩		0887	vy lt tan
	498	◩		047	lt red
◆	500		◩	0879	spruce
△	519	◩		0168	turquoise
▲	610			0889	vy dk tan
8	642	◩		0832	dk beige
	644	◩		0831	beige
2	646			0400	dk grey
◇	647		◩	0900	grey
B	648	◩		8581	lt grey
S	676	◩		0874	lt gold
4	677	◩		0292	vy lt gold
△	680			0901	dk gold
☆	729	◩		0890	gold
5	754	◩		4146	peach
⊙	761	◩		08	pink
*	814			044	dk red
C	815	◩		043	red
+	822	◩		0830	lt beige
★	844			0401	vy dk grey
✦	869	◩	◩	0906	dk tan
3	902			022	vy dk red
+	930			0922	dk blue
A	931			0921	blue
	932			0920	lt blue
−	948	◩		0892	lt peach
E	3045	◩		0888	lt tan
V	3072	◩		0847	vy lt grey
R	3347			0265	yellow green
●	blanc				white French Knot
●	310				black French Knot

Grey area indicates last row of top section of design.

JOY SANTA (105w x 149h)			
Aida 11	9⅝"	x	13⅝"
Aida 14	7½"	x	10¾"
Aida 18	5⅞"	x	8⅜"
Hardanger 22	4⅞"	x	6⅞"

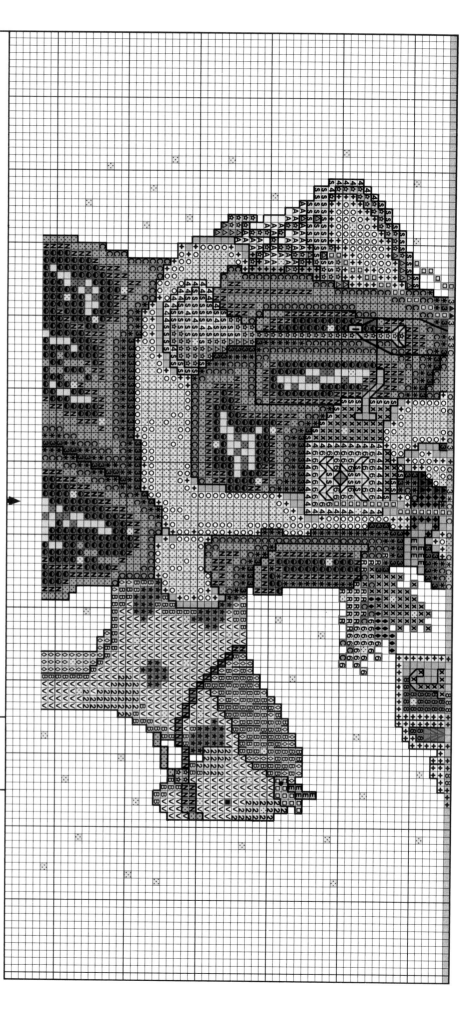

Joy Santa (shown on page 55): The design was stitched on a 16" x 19" piece of Indigo Aida (14 ct). Three strands of floss were used for Cross Stitch and 1 for Backstitch and French Knots. It was custom framed.

The upper portion **only** of Santa (refer to photo on page 54) was also stitched over two fabric threads on a 12" square of Dutch Blue Cashel Linen (28 ct). Three strands of floss were used for Cross Stitch and 1 for Backstitch and French Knots. It was inserted in a custom frame and applied to a wreath.

Design by Sandi Gore Evans.

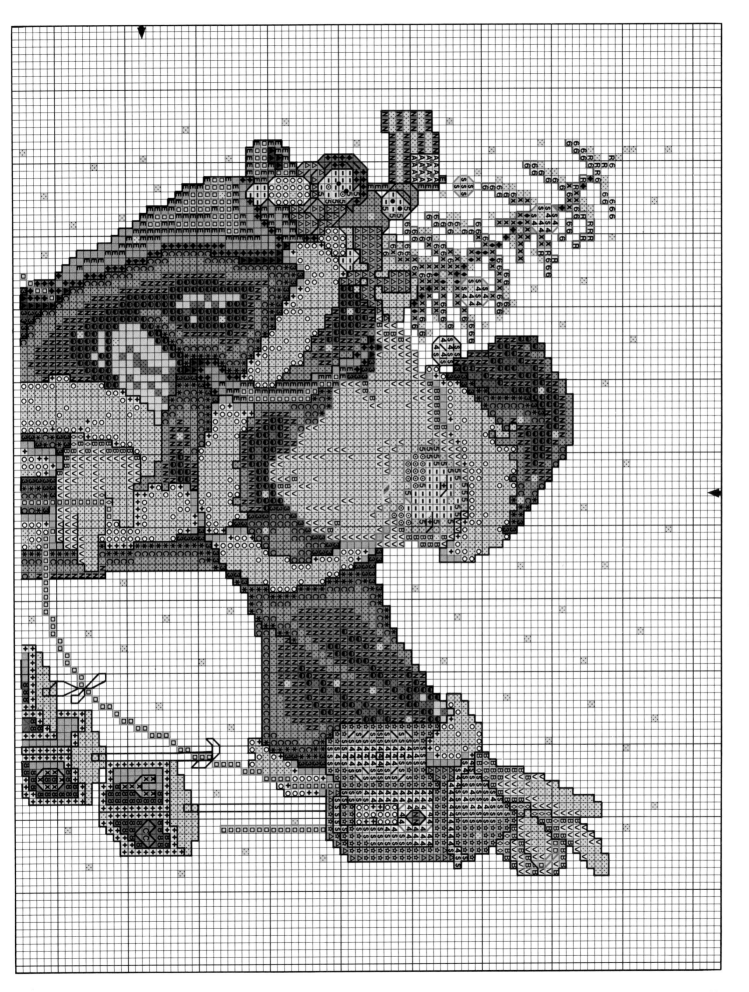

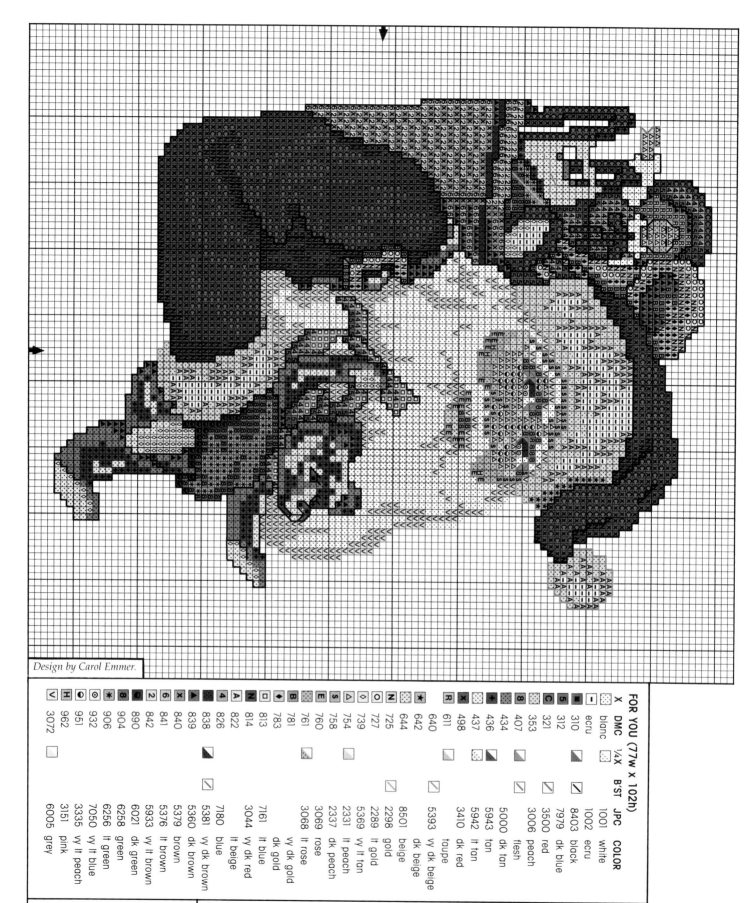

Design by Carol Emmer.

FOR YOU (77w x 102h)

DMC	JPC	COLOR
blanc	1001	white
ecru	1002	ecru
310	8403	black
312	7979	dk blue
321	3500	red
353	3006	peach
498	3410	dk red
437	5942	lt tan
436	5943	tan
434	5000	dk tan
407		flesh
611	5393	toupe
640		vy dk beige
642		dk beige
644	8501	beige
725	2298	gold
727	2289	lt gold
739	5369	vy lt tan
754	2331	lt peach
758	2337	dk peach
760	3069	rose
761	3068	lt rose
781		vy dk gold
783		dk gold
813	7161	lt blue
814		vy dk red
838	3044	vy dk brown
826	5381	blue
822	7180	lt beige
839	5360	dk brown
840	5379	brown
841	5376	lt brown
842	5933	vy lt brown
890	6021	dk green
904	6258	green
906	6256	lt green
932	7050	vy lt blue
951	3335	vy lt peach
962	351	pink
3072	6005	grey

(Key columns: X, DMC, ¼X, B'ST, JPC, COLOR)

FOR YOU (77w x 102h)

Aida 11	7"	x	9⅜"
Aida 14	5½"	x	7⅜"
Aida 18	4⅜"	x	5¾"
Hardanger 22	3½"	x	4¾"

For You (shown on page 57): The design was stitched over two fabric threads on a 13" x 15" piece of Cream Belfast Linen (32 ct). Two strands of floss were used for Cross Stitch and 1 for Backstitch. It was custom framed.

The design (shown on page 56) was also stitched on a prefinished Gold & Cream Tilla (10 ct) tree skirt. Five strands of floss were used for Cross Stitch and 2 for Backstitch.

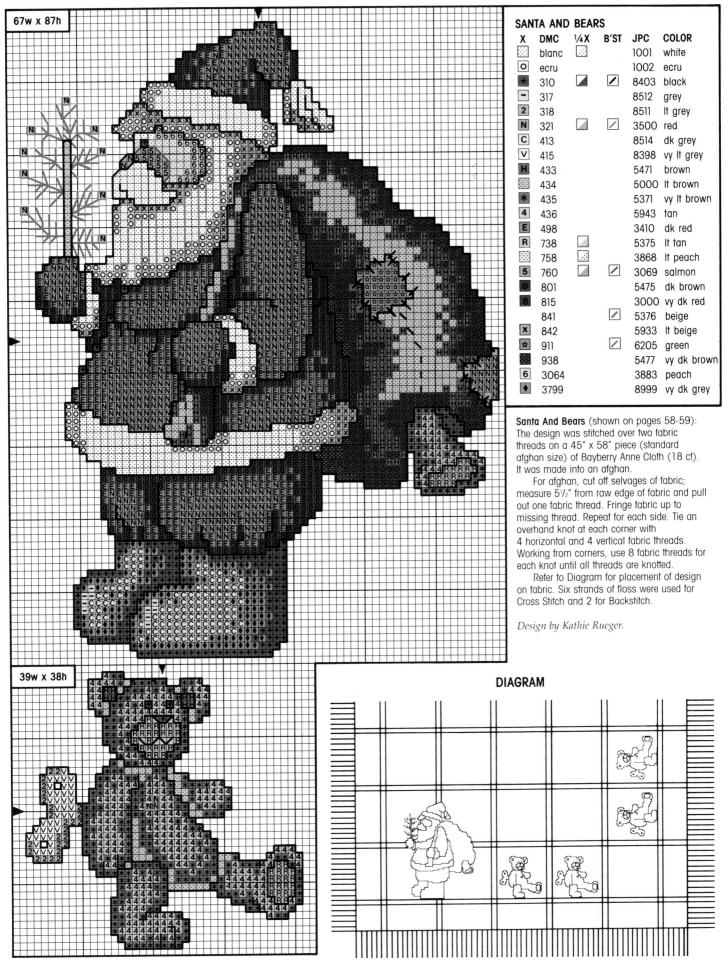

67w x 87h

39w x 38h

SANTA AND BEARS

X	DMC	1/4X	B'ST	JPC	COLOR
	blanc			1001	white
O	ecru			1002	ecru
+	310		/	8403	black
-	317			8512	grey
2	318			8511	lt grey
N	321		/	3500	red
C	413			8514	dk grey
V	415			8398	vy lt grey
H	433			5471	brown
	434			5000	lt brown
*	435			5371	vy lt brown
4	436			5943	tan
E	498			3410	dk red
R	738			5375	lt tan
	758			3868	lt peach
5	760		/	3069	salmon
	801			5475	dk brown
8	815			3000	vy dk red
	841		/	5376	beige
X	842			5933	lt beige
☆	911		/	6205	green
	938			5477	vy dk brown
6	3064			3883	peach
◆	3799			8999	vy dk grey

Santa And Bears (shown on pages 58-59): The design was stitched over two fabric threads on a 45" x 58" piece (standard afghan size) of Bayberry Anne Cloth (18 ct). It was made into an afghan.

For afghan, cut off selvages of fabric; measure 5¹/₂" from raw edge of fabric and pull out one fabric thread. Fringe fabric up to missing thread. Repeat for each side. Tie an overhand knot at each corner with 4 horizontal and 4 vertical fabric threads. Working from corners, use 8 fabric threads for each knot until all threads are knotted.

Refer to Diagram for placement of design on fabric. Six strands of floss were used for Cross Stitch and 2 for Backstitch.

Design by Kathie Rueger.

DIAGRAM

133

MERRY GENTLEMEN (170w x 101h)

X	DMC	¼X	B'ST	COLOR	X	DMC	¼X	B'ST	COLOR	X	DMC	¼X	½X	B'ST	COLOR
	blanc		/	white		500		/	vy dk green		760				salmon
	ecru			ecru		501			dk green		814				dk maroon
-	309			rose		502			green		816				red
	310		/	black		503			lt green		839			/	dk beige
	315			dk mauve	4	504			vy lt green		840				beige
	316			lt mauve		676		/	yellow	3	841				lt beige
S	326			dk rose	2	729			gold		842				vy lt beige
★	335			lt rose		754			lt peach		902				vy dk mauve
	420			dk gold		758			peach		3685				maroon

134

X	DMC	¼X	B'ST	COLOR
■	3726	◢		mauve
◇	3727	◢		vy lt mauve
	3781		◢	brown
●	310			black French Knot
⊘	310			black Lazy Daisy Stitch
●	00161			crystal Mill Hill Glass Seed Bead
●	03015			snow white Mill Hill Antique Seed Bead
●	03003			cranberry Mill Hill Antique Seed Bead
●	03035			royal green Mill Hill Antique Seed Bead
▨				Grey area indicates last row of right section of design.

Merry Gentlemen (shown on pages 62-63): The design was stitched over two fabric threads on a 22" x 17" piece of Mushroom Lugana (25 ct). Three strands of floss were used for Cross Stitch and 1 for Half Cross Stitch, Backstitch, French Knots, and Lazy Daisy Stitches. It was custom framed.

Each Santa (shown on pages 62-63) was also stitched separately over two fabric threads on a 9" x 12" piece of Ivory Aida (14 ct). Six strands of floss were used for Cross Stitch and 2 for Half Cross Stitch, Backstitch, French Knots, and Lazy Daisy Stitches. See Stuffed Figure Finishing, page 141.

Design by Marilyn Gandré.
Needlework adaptation by Nancy Dockter.

TURN-OF-THE-CENTURY SANTA
(62w x 103h)

X	DMC	¼X	B'ST	ANC.	COLOR
⠂	blanc	⠂		2	white
◐	300			352	vy dk rust
▨	301			1049	rust
■	310	◩	╱	403	black
⊠	311	◩		148	vy dk blue
⊞	312	◩		979	dk blue
▨	318	◩		399	grey
⬠	321	◩	╱	9046	lt red
✳	322		╱	978	blue
═	334			977	lt blue
─	353			6	flesh
▼	400			351	dk rust
✦	402			1047	vy lt rust
▲	414	◩		235	dk grey
─	415	◩		398	lt grey
◈	420			374	dk tan
⊠	422	◩		373	lt tan
◻	498	◩		1005	red
◆	645			273	vy dk grey
★	699		╱	923	dk green
▨	701			227	green
▽	703	▽		238	lt green
○	725		▢	305	yellow
▼	726			295	lt yellow
◆	739	▢		387	vy lt tan
⠿	754	⠿		1012	lt flesh
▽	760	◩	╱	1022	pink
◉	761			1021	lt pink
▢	783			307	dk yellow
★	814			45	dk red
⬠	839	◩	╱	360	brown
✳	922			1003	lt rust
◑	951			1010	vy lt flesh
✕	3045	◩		888	tan
	3064		╱	883	dk flesh
★	3072			847	vy lt grey
▢	3325			129	vy lt blue
•	310		black French Knot		
╱	321		lt red Lazy Daisy Stitch		

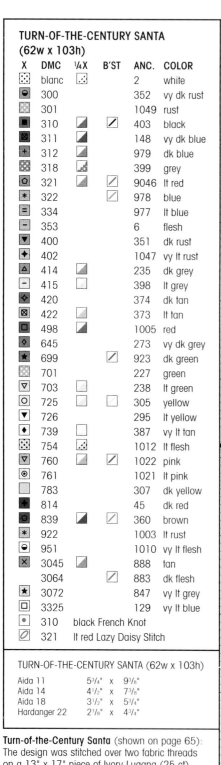

TURN-OF-THE-CENTURY SANTA (62w x 103h)

Aida 11	5³⁄₄"	x	9³⁄₈"
Aida 14	4¹⁄₂"	x	7³⁄₈"
Aida 18	3¹⁄₂"	x	5³⁄₄"
Hardanger 22	2⁷⁄₈"	x	4³⁄₄"

Turn-of-the-Century Santa (shown on page 65): The design was stitched over two fabric threads on a 13" x 17" piece of Ivory Lugana (25 ct). Three strands of floss were used for Cross Stitch and 1 for Backstitch, French Knots, and Lazy Daisy Stitches. It was custom framed.

Santa's face **only** (refer to photo on page 65) was also stitched over two fabric threads on a 6" square of Ivory Lugana (25 ct). Three strands of floss were used for Cross Stitch and 1 for Backstitch. See Mini Pillow Finishing, page 141.

The top portion **only** of the design (refer to photo on page 64) was stitched over two fabric threads on an 18" x 8" piece of Ivory Lugana (25 ct). Three strands of floss were used for Cross Stitch and 1 for Backstitch. It was made into a stocking cuff. Continued on page 142.

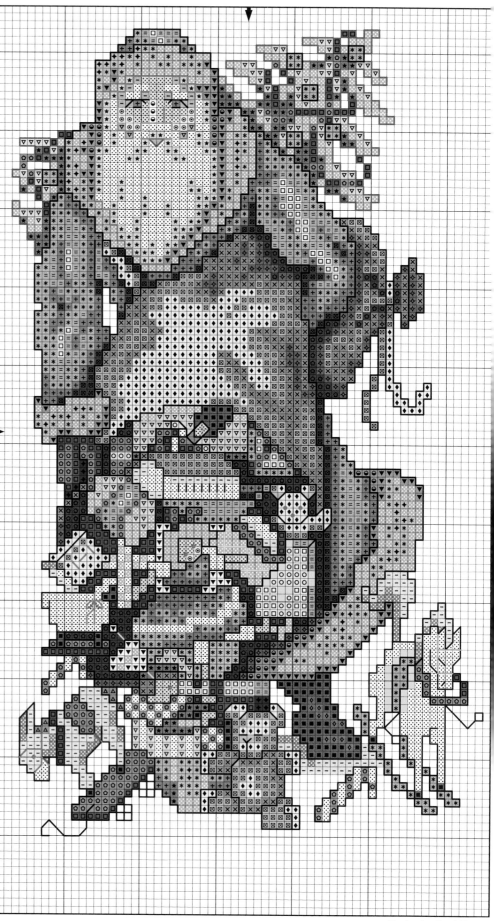

Design by Carol Emmer.

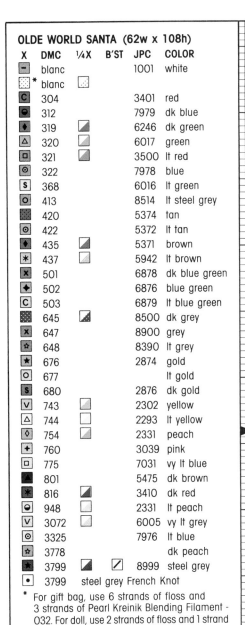

OLDE WORLD SANTA (62w x 108h)

X	DMC	¼X	B'ST	JPC	COLOR
-	blanc			1001	white
*	blanc				
C	304			3401	red
⊙	312			7979	dk blue
◆	319	◺		6246	dk green
△	320	◺		6017	green
□	321	◺		3500	lt red
⊙	322			7978	blue
S	368			6016	lt green
O	413			8514	lt steel grey
▦	420			5374	tan
⊙	422			5372	lt tan
◆	435	◺		5371	brown
*	437	◺		5942	lt brown
X	501			6878	dk blue green
✦	502			6876	blue green
C	503			6879	lt blue green
▦	645	◺		8500	dk grey
X	647			8900	grey
☆	648			8390	lt grey
★	676			2874	gold
◎	677				lt gold
S	680			2876	dk gold
V	743	◺		2302	yellow
△	744	◻		2293	lt yellow
◇	754	◺		2331	peach
+	760			3039	pink
▣	775			7031	vy lt blue
▦	801			5475	dk brown
*	816	◣		3410	dk red
⊙	948	◻		2331	lt peach
V	3072	◺		6005	vy lt grey
⊙	3325			7976	lt blue
☆	3778				dk peach
★	3799	◣	╱	8999	steel grey
•	3799		steel grey French Knot		

* For gift bag, use 6 strands of floss and
3 strands of Pearl Kreinik Blending Filament -
032. For doll, use 2 strands of floss and 1 strand
of Pearl Kreinik Blending Filament - 032.

Olde World Santa (shown on page 67): The design was stitched over two fabric threads on a 19½" x 32¼" piece of Cracked Wheat Ragusa (14 ct). Six strands of floss were used for Cross Stitch and 2 for Backstitch and French Knots. It was made into a gift bag.

For gift bag, cut a piece of Ragusa same size as stitched piece. Matching right sides and raw edges, use a ½" seam allowance to sew along side and bottom edges. For boxed corners, fold each bottom corner to a point, matching side and bottom seamlines. Stitch across each corner 2" from point of corner. Turn top edge of bag ¼" to wrong side and press. Turn ½" to wrong side and hem. Turn gift bag right side out.

The design (shown on page 66) was also stitched on a 9" x 12" piece of Ivory Aida (14 ct). Three strands of floss were used for Cross Stitch and 1 for Backstitch and French Knots. It was made into a stuffed figure.

For stuffed figure, cut a 9" x 12" piece of Ivory Aida (14 ct) for backing. Matching right sides and raw edges and leaving bottom edge open, sew stitched piece and backing together ¼" from

OLDE WORLD SANTA (62w x 108h)

14 count	4½"	x	7¾"
16 count	3⅞"	x	6¾"
18 count	3½"	x	6"
22 count	2⅞"	x	5"

design. Trim bottom edge of figure 1" away from design. Leaving a ¼" seam allowance, cut out figure. Clip seam allowances at curves; turn figure right side out and carefully push curves outward. Press raw edges ⅜" to wrong side; stuff figure with polyester fiberfill up to 1½" from opening.

For base, set figure on tracing paper and draw around base of figure. Add a ½" seam allowance to pattern; cut out. Place pattern on piece of Aida. Use fabric marking pen to draw around pattern; cut out along drawn line. Baste around base piece ½"

from raw edge; press raw edges to wrong side along basting line.

To weight bottom of figure, fill a plastic sandwich bag with a small amount of aquarium gravel. Place bag of gravel into opening of figure.

Pin wrong side of base piece over opening. Whipstitch in place, adding polyester fiberfill as necessary to fill bottom of figure. Remove basting threads.

Design by Lorraine Birmingham.

137

Dear Santa (shown on pages 68-69): The design was stitched on a 15" x 22" piece of Delft Blue Aida (14 ct). Three strands of floss were used for Cross Stitch and 1 for Backstitch and French Knots. It was custom framed.

Design by D. Morgan.

DEAR SANTA (97w x 189h)

Aida 11	8⅞"	x	17¼"
Aida 14	7"	x	13½"
Aida 18	5½"	x	10½"
Hardanger 22	4½"	x	8⅝"

DEAR SANTA (97w x 189h)

X	DMC	¼X	B'ST	ANC.	COLOR	X	DMC	¼X	B'ST	ANC.	COLOR
⊡	blanc	⊡	╱*	2	white	+	816	◢		1005	lt red
■	310	◢	╱	403	black	◆	890	◢		218	dk green
▽	319	◢		218	green	✕	930	◢		1035	blue
○	320			215	lt green	◉	931			1034	lt blue
✳	415	◢		398	grey	△	3350	◢		59	lt rose
⊠	433	◢		358	brown	◆	3685	◢		1028	rose
☆	434			310	lt brown	●	310				black French Knot
−	743			302	yellow	*Work in long stitches.					
○	745			300	lt yellow	▨ Grey area indicates last row					
☻	762		╱	234	lt grey	of top section of design.					
▣	815	◢		43	red						

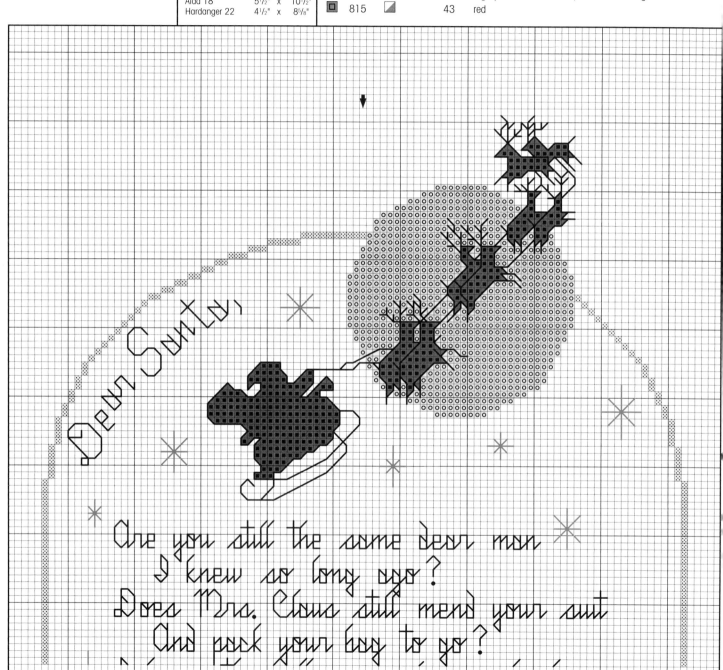

I knew the bells on reindeer hoof
And felt the snow crunch on my roof.
I ran to peek in at the tree.
(That breathless little child was me.)
How marvelously jolly round—
You stilled my heart without a sound.
How quiet you were beside the tree—
You drank the cocoa there from me.
Now with values rearranged,
Please don't tell me you have changed.
Does Mrs. Claus still mend your suit
And pack your bag to go?
Are you still the same dear man
I knew so long ago?

GENERAL INSTRUCTIONS
WORKING WITH CHARTS

How to Read Charts: Each of the designs is shown in chart form. Each colored square on the chart represents one Cross Stitch or one Half Cross Stitch. Each colored triangle on the chart represents one One-Quarter Stitch or one Three-Quarter Stitch. Black or colored dots represent French Knots. Black or colored ovals represent Lazy Daisy Stitches. The straight lines on the chart indicate Backstitch. When a French Knot, Lazy Daisy Stitch, or Backstitch covers a square, the symbol is omitted.

Each chart is accompanied by a color key. This key indicates the color of floss to use for each stitch on the chart. The headings on the color key are for Cross Stitch (**X**), DMC color number (**DMC**), One-Quarter Stitch (**¼X**), Three-Quarter Stitch (**¾X**), Half Cross Stitch (**½X**), Backstitch (**B'ST**), J. & P. Coats color number (**JPC**), Anchor color number (**ANC**), and color name (**COLOR**). Color key columns should be read vertically and horizontally to determine type of stitch and floss color.

How to Determine Finished Size: The finished size of your design will depend on the thread count per inch of the fabric being used. To determine the finished size of the design on different fabrics, divide the number of squares (stitches) in the width of the charted design by the thread count of the fabric. For example, a charted design with a width of 80 squares worked on 14 count Aida will yield a design 5¾" wide. Repeat for the number of squares (stitches) in the height of the charted design. (**Note:** To work over two fabric threads, divide the number of squares by one-half the thread count.) Then add the amount of background you want plus a generous amount for finishing.

Where to Start: The horizontal and vertical centers of the charted design are shown by arrows. You may start at any point on the charted design, but be sure the design will be centered on the fabric. Locate the center of fabric by folding in half, top to bottom and again left to right. On the charted design, count the number of squares from the center of the chart to the determined starting point; then from the fabric's center, count out the same number of fabric threads.

STITCH DIAGRAMS

Counted Cross Stitch (X): Work a Cross Stitch to correspond to each colored square on the chart. For horizontal rows, work stitches in two journeys (**Fig. 1**). For vertical rows, complete each stitch as shown (**Fig. 2**). When working over two fabric threads, work Cross Stitch as shown in **Fig. 3**. When the chart shows a Backstitch crossing a colored square (**Fig. 4**), a Cross Stitch should be worked first; then the Backstitch (**Fig. 9 or 10**) should be worked on top of the Cross Stitch.

Fig. 1   **Fig. 2**

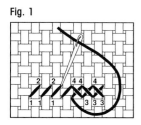   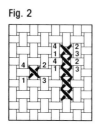

Fig. 3 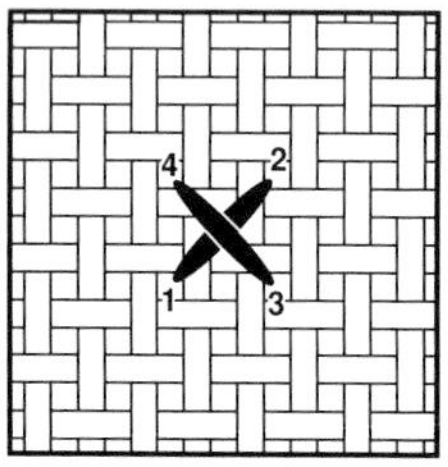   **Fig. 4**

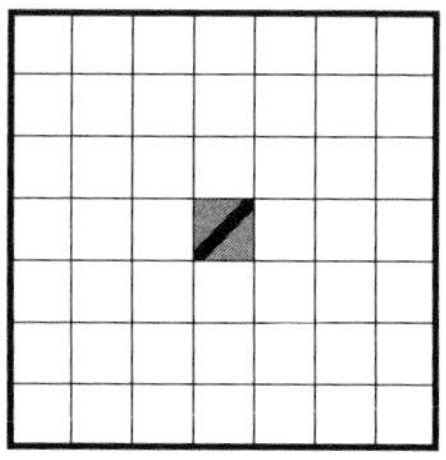

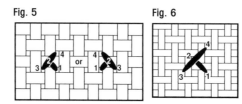

Quarter Stitch (¼X and ¾X): Quarter Stitches are denoted by triangular shapes of color on the chart and on the color key. Come up at 1 (**Fig. 5**); then split fabric thread to go down at 2. When stitches 1-4 are worked in the same color, the resulting stitch is called a Three-Quarter Stitch (**¾X**). **Fig. 6** shows the technique for Quarter Stitches when working over two fabric threads.

Fig. 5   **Fig. 6**

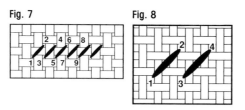

Half Cross Stitch (½X): This stitch is one journey of the Cross Stitch and is worked from lower left to upper right as shown in **Fig. 7**. When working over two fabric threads, work Half Cross Stitch as shown in **Fig. 8**.

Fig. 7   **Fig. 8**

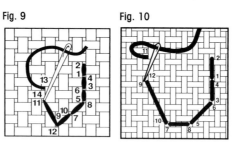

Backstitch (B'ST): For outline detail, Backstitch (shown on chart and on color key by black or colored straight lines) should be worked after the design has been completed (**Fig. 9**). When working over two fabric threads, work Backstitch as shown in **Fig. 10**.

Fig. 9   **Fig. 10**

French Knot: Bring needle up at 1. Wrap floss once around needle and insert needle at 2, holding end of floss with non-stitching fingers (**Fig. 11**). Tighten knot; then pull needle through fabric, holding floss until it must be released. For larger knot, use more strands; wrap only once.

Fig. 11

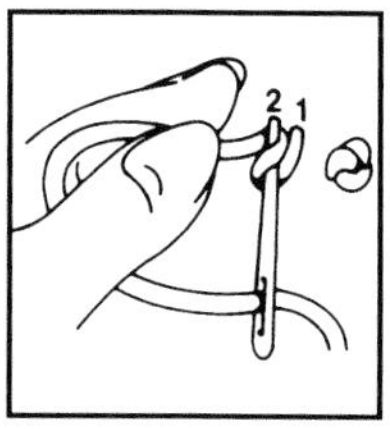

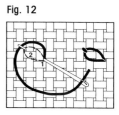

Lazy Daisy Stitch: Bring needle up at 1 and make a loop. Go down at 1 and come up at 2, keeping floss below point of needle (**Fig. 12**). Pull needle through and go down at 2 to anchor loop, completing stitch. (**Note:** To support stitches, it may be helpful to go down in edge of next fabric thread when anchoring loop.)

Fig. 12

STITCHING TIP

Working over Two Fabric Threads: Use the sewing method instead of the stab method when working over two fabric threads. To use the sewing method, keep your stitching hand on the right side of the fabric (instead of stabbing the fabric with the needle and taking your stitching hand to the back of the fabric to pick up the needle). With the sewing method, you take the needle down and up with one stroke instead of two. To add support to stitches, it is important that the first Cross Stitch is placed on the fabric with stitch 1-2 beginning and ending where a vertical fabric thread crosses over a horizontal fabric thread (**Fig. 13**). When the first stitch is in the correct position, the entire design will be placed properly, with vertical fabric threads supporting each stitch.

Fig. 13

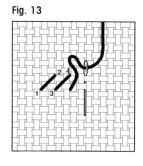

FINISHING TECHNIQUES

AFGHAN FINISHING

Step 1. Cut off selvages. Fabric should measure 45"w x 58"l. For fringe, measure 5 1/2" from raw edge of fabric and pull out one fabric thread. Beginning at raw edge of fabric, unravel fabric up to missing fabric thread. Repeat for each side. Using overhand knots, begin by tying a knot at each corner with four horizontal and four vertical fabric threads (**Fig. 14**). Working from the corners, use eight fabric threads for each knot until all threads are knotted.

Fig. 14

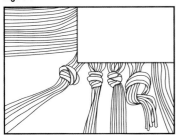

Step 2. Refer to Diagram to stitch design.

Diagram

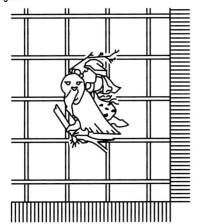

PILLOW FINISHING

1. For pillow top, trim stitched piece to desired size plus 1/2" on all sides for seam allowances. Cut pillow backing same size as pillow top.

2. To make cording, cut a bias strip of fabric 2"w and outer dimension of pillow top plus 1". (**Note:** This strip may be pieced if necessary.) Lay purchased cord along center of strip on wrong side of fabric; fold strip over cord. Use zipper foot to machine baste along length of strip close to cord.

3. To make ruffle, cut a strip of fabric twice desired finished width plus 1" for seam allowances and twice outer dimension of pillow top (measure edges of pillow top; then double measurement). (**Note:** This strip may be pieced if necessary.) Press short ends 1/2" to wrong side. Fold strip in half lengthwise with wrong sides together and press. Baste close to raw edge. Make another basting seam 1/4" from the first. Pull basting threads, drawing up gathers to fit pillow top.

4. For cording, start at bottom edge of pillow top and 1" from end of cording. Baste cording to right side of pillow top with finished edge toward center of pillow and raw edges facing outward. Opening ends of cording, cut cord to fit exactly. Insert one end of cording in the other; turn top end under 1/2" and baste in place. Use zipper foot to sew cording in place along seam line.

For ruffle, start at bottom edge of pillow top and sew ruffle to right side of pillow top with finished edge toward center of pillow and gathered edges facing outward. Join ends of ruffle using blind stitches.

5. Matching right sides and raw edges, use a 1/2" seam allowance to sew pillow backing to pillow top, leaving an opening at bottom edge. Clip seam allowances at corners and curves. Turn pillow right side out, carefully pushing corners and curves outward. Stuff pillow with polyester fiberfill; sew final closure by hand.

MINI PILLOW FINISHING: With design centered on fabric, cut stitched piece and backing fabric (same fabric as stitched piece) desired width and height plus 1/2" on all four sides to allow for fringe. Matching wrong sides and raw edges, use desired floss color to cross stitch fabric pieces together 1/2" from bottom and side edges. Stuff pillow with polyester fiberfill. Cross stitch across top of pillow 1/2" from edges. Fringe fabric to one square from cross-stitched lines. If desired, whipstitch ribbon to pillow for hanger.

STUFFED FIGURE FINISHING: For stuffed figure, cut backing fabric (same fabric as stitched piece) the same size as stitched piece. Matching right sides and raw edges and leaving bottom edge open, sew stitched piece and backing fabric together 1/4" from design. Trim bottom edge of figure 1" away from design. Leaving a 1/4" seam allowance, cut out figure. Clip seam allowances at curves. Turn figure right side out, carefully pushing curves outward. Press raw edges 3/8" to wrong side; stuff figure with polyester fiberfill up to 1 1/2" from opening.

For base, set figure on tracing paper and draw around base of figure. Add a 1/2" seam allowance to pattern; cut out. Place pattern on piece of same fabric as stitched piece. Use fabric marking pen to draw around pattern; cut out along drawn line. Baste around base piece 1/2" from raw edge; press raw edges to wrong side along basting line.

To weight bottom of figure, fill a plastic sandwich bag with a small amount of aquarium gravel. Place bag of gravel into opening of figure.

Pin wrong side of base piece over opening. Whipstitch in place, adding polyester fiberfill as necessary to fill bottom of figure. Remove basting threads.

Father Christmas

Continued from page 87.
Project shown on page 16.

For ruffle, cut a 6 yd long by 7" wide piece of fabric, piecing as necessary. With wrong sides together, fold fabric in half lengthwise and press. To gather fabric, baste close to raw edge; make another basting seam 1/4" from the first. Pull basting threads, drawing up gathers to fit outer edge of skirt. Baste ruffle to outer edge of right side of skirt top with folded edge toward center of skirt and raw edges even.

With right sides facing and leaving an opening for turning, use a 1/2" seam allowance and sew skirt top and backing together. Clip curves; turn right side out and press. Sew final closure by hand.

Referring to photo, sew a 4 yd length of 1/2" w upholstery trim to right side of skirt at top of ruffle.

For stitched piece oval pattern, fold a 7" x 10 1/2" piece of tissue paper in half from bottom to top and again from left to right. Referring to **Fig. 15**, draw a one-quarter circle at corner of paper; cut out pattern. Unfold pattern and press to flatten.

Fig. 15

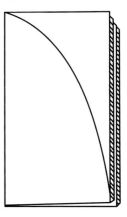

Center pattern on wrong side of stitched piece and draw around pattern; remove pattern and cut out stitched piece. Center stitched piece on top of skirt (on opposite side of slit in skirt) and baste in place. Sew a 32" length of 1/2" w upholstery trim around outer edge of stitched piece, sewing stitched piece to skirt at the same time.

Wayfaring Santa

Continued from page 89.
Project shown on page 88.
Stocking pattern shown in black on page 144.

Matching arrows to form one pattern, trace entire stocking pattern onto tracing paper; cut out pattern. Referring to photo for placement, place pattern over design on wrong side of stitched piece; pin pattern in place. Use fabric marking pen to draw around pattern. Do **not** cut out.

With right sides facing and matching raw edges, pin stitched piece and backing fabric together. Leaving top edge open, sew stitched piece and backing fabric together directly on drawn line. Trim seam allowance to 1/2" and clip curves. Trim top edge along drawn line.

Repeat to draw around pattern and sew lining pieces together, sewing just inside drawn lines and leaving top edge open. Trim seam allowance to 1/2" and clip curves. Trim top edge along drawn line. **Do not turn lining right side out.** Press top edge of lining 1/2" to wrong side.

With right sides facing and matching short edges, fold each cuff piece in half. Using a 1/2" seam allowance, sew along short edges of each piece.

For cording, cut one 2" x 15 1/2" bias strip of coordinating fabric. Center cord on wrong side of bias strip; matching long edges, fold strip over cord. Using zipper foot, baste along length of strip close to cord; trim seam allowance to 1/2". Matching raw edges and beginning at cuff seam, pin cording to right side of one cuff piece. Ends of cording should overlap approx. 2"; pin overlapping end out of the way.

Starting 2" from beginning end of cording and ending 4" from overlapping end, baste cording to cuff piece.

On overlapping end of cording, remove 2 1/2" of basting; fold end of fabric back and trim cord so that it meets beginning end of cord. Fold end of fabric under 1/2"; wrap fabric over beginning end of cording. Finish basting cording to cuff piece. With right sides facing and matching raw edges, use a zipper foot and 1/2" seam allowance to sew cuff pieces together along edge with cording. Turn right side out and press.

With right side of cuff (side with cording) and wrong side of stocking facing, match raw edges and use a 1/2" seam allowance to sew cuff to stocking. Fold cuff 3 1/4" over stocking; press.

For hanger, cut one 1" x 6" strip of coordinating fabric. Press each long edge of strip 1/4" to center. Matching long edges, fold strip in half and sew close to folded edges. Matching short edges, fold strip in half and whipstitch to inside of stocking at left seam.

With wrong sides facing and matching edges, place lining inside stocking. Matching pressed edge of lining to seam of cuff, whipstitch lining to stocking.

Santa In Blue

Continued from page 95.
Project shown on page 20.
Stocking pattern shown in blue on page 144.

For stocking, cut backing fabric and two pieces of fabric for lining same size as stitched piece. Cut one 12" x 7" piece of coordinating fabric for cuff.

Trace stocking pattern onto tracing paper adding 4" to height of stocking; cut out pattern. Place pattern over stitched piece (see photo, page 20, for placement) and mark edge at top, heel, and toe with a pin. Turn stitched piece and pattern over and match pattern to pins. Use fabric marking pen to draw around pattern. Draw around pattern on wrong side of one lining piece.

With right sides facing, pin stitched piece and backing fabric together. Leaving top edge open, carefully sew stitched piece and backing fabric together directly on drawn line; trim top along drawn line. Leaving a 1/4" seam allowance, cut out stocking. Clip seam allowance at curves. Turn stocking right side out.

With right sides facing, pin lining pieces together. Leaving top edge open, carefully sew lining pieces together 1/8" inside drawn line; trim top along drawn line. Leaving a 1/4" seam allowance, cut out lining. Clip seam allowance at curves. **Do not turn right side out.**

With wrong sides together and matching raw edges, place lining inside stocking. Using a 1/4" seam allowance, baste stocking and lining together around top edge.

For hanger, fold a 7" length of 3/8"w ribbon in half. Matching raw edges, pin ribbon to inside of stocking at left seam.

For cuff, fold a 12" x 7" piece of fabric in half, with right sides together and matching short edges. Sew 1/4" from short edges; press seam open. Turn fabric right side out. With wrong sides together and matching long edges, fold fabric in half; press.

Matching raw edges, pin cuff inside stocking (cuff seam should be at center back of stocking). Using a 3/8" seam allowance, sew stocking and cuff together. Fold cuff to outside of stocking, leaving seam inside stocking; press fold.

Santa's Journey

Continued from page 97.
Project shown on page 96.

For wall hanging, measure 2 1/2" from bottom of design and pull out one horizontal fabric thread. Fringe up to missing thread. On each long edge, turn fabric 1/2" to wrong side and press; turn 1/2" to wrong side again and hem. Trim fringe to 2 3/4". For casing at top edge, turn fabric 1/2" to wrong side and press; turn 2" to wrong side again and hem. Insert stick in casing.

Turn-of-the-Century Santa

Continued from page 136.
Project shown on page 64.
Stocking pattern on page 143.

For stocking, cut two 14" x 20" pieces of fabric. Cut two 14" x 20" pieces of fabric for lining.

Matching arrows to form one pattern, trace entire stocking pattern onto tracing paper; cut out pattern. Place pattern on wrong side of stocking fabric; pin pattern in place. Use fabric marking pen to draw around pattern. Do **not** cut out.

With right sides facing and matching raw edges, pin stocking fabric pieces together. Leaving top edge open, sew stocking fabric pieces together directly on drawn line. Trim seam allowance to 1/2" and clip curves. Trim top edge along drawn line. Turn right side out and press.

Repeat to draw around pattern and sew lining pieces together, sewing just inside drawn lines, leaving top edge open, and leaving a 4" opening along one side seam for turning. Trim seam allowance to 1/2" and clip curves. Trim top edge along drawn line. **Do not turn lining right side out.**

For cuff, center design and trim stitched piece to 15 1/4"w x 5 1/4"h. Cut a piece of fabric the same size as stitched piece for lining. With right sides facing and matching short edges, fold cuff and cuff lining piece in half. Using a 1/2" seam allowance, sew along short edges of each piece.

For cording, cut two 2" x 16 1/2" bias strips of coordinating fabric. Center cord on wrong side of each bias strip; matching long edges fold strip over cord. Using zipper foot, baste along length of each strip close to cord; trim seam allowances to 1/2". Matching raw edges and beginning at cuff seam, pin cording to right side of bottom edge of cuff piece. Ends of cording should overlap approx. 2"; pin overlapping end out of the way.

Starting 2" from beginning end of cording and ending 4" from overlapping end, baste cording to cuff piece.

On overlapping end of cording, remove 2 1/2" of basting; fold end of fabric back and trim cord so that it meets beginning end of cord. Fold end of fabric under 1/2"; wrap fabric over beginning end of cording. Finish basting cording to cuff. With right sides facing and matching raw edges, use a zipper foot and 1/2" seam allowance to sew cuff and cuff lining piece together along edge with cording. Turn right side out and press.

With wrong side of cuff and right side of stocking facing, match raw edges and baste cuff to stocking. Follow previous instructions to baste remaining cording to top edge of cuff.

For hanger, cut one 1 1/2" x 6" strip of coordinating fabric. Press each long edge of strip 1/4" to center. Matching long edges, fold strip in half and sew close to folded edges. Matching raw edges, fold strip in half and baste to cuff on left side.

With right sides facing and matching raw edges, insert stocking inside lining. Using a 1/2" seam allowance, stitch through all layers to sew lining to stocking. Turn right side out through opening in lining; sew final closure by hand. Insert lining inside stocking; press.

SANTA

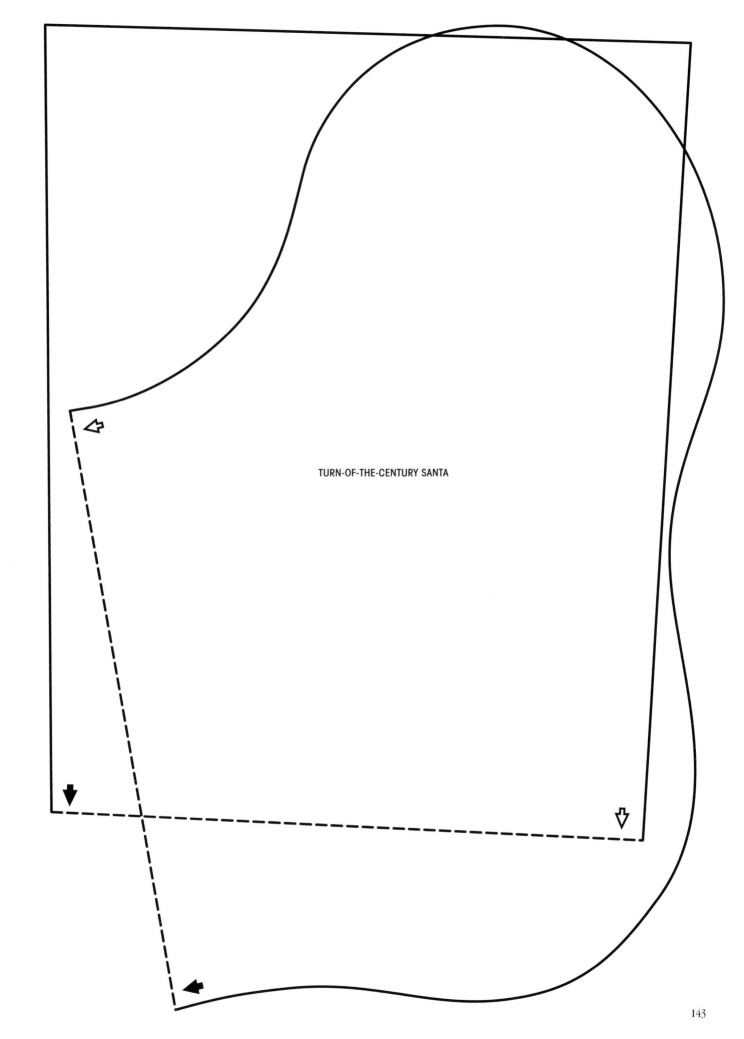

TURN-OF-THE-CENTURY SANTA

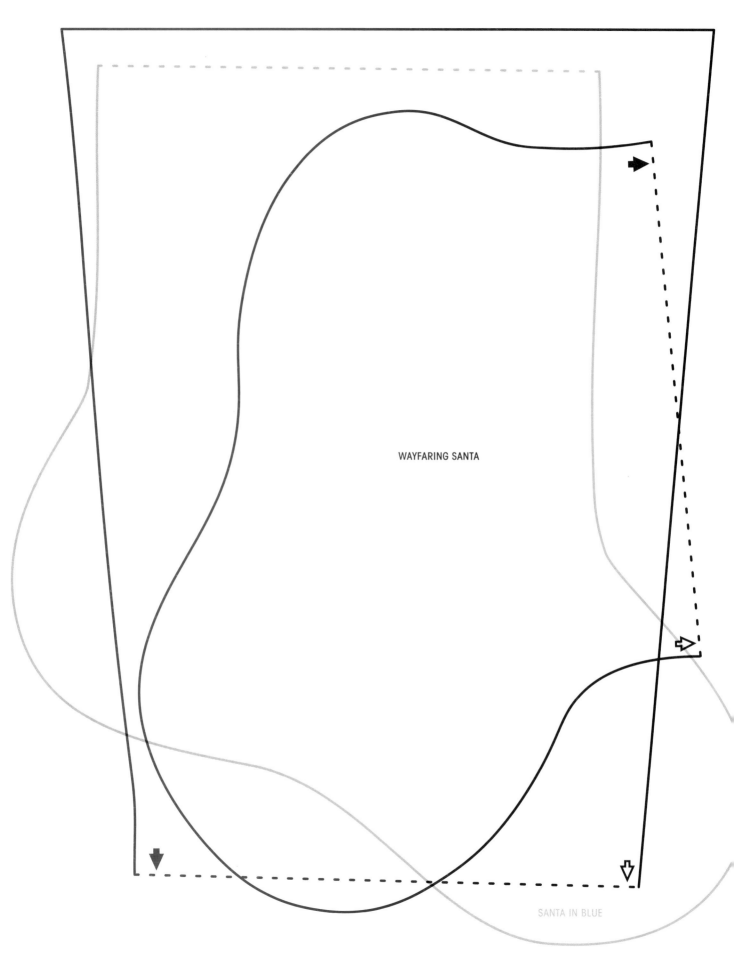

WAYFARING SANTA

SANTA IN BLUE